LEARN HTML

100+ Coding Q&A

Yasin Cakal

Code Of Code

CONTENTS

INTRODUCTION

Welcome to the Learn HTML course! If you're interested in learning how to create and design websites, then this course is for you. HTML, or Hypertext Markup Language, is the standard markup language for creating web pages. It provides the structure and content for websites, making it an essential skill for any web developer.

In this course, you will learn the basics of HTML, including how to structure an HTML document, format text, add images and links, and create forms. You'll also learn advanced techniques like working with frames and iframes, using HTML5 semantic tags, and creating multimedia content.

Throughout the course, you'll get hands-on experience by building a complete HTML website as a final project. By the end of this course, you'll have the skills and knowledge you need to create your own professional-quality websites.

So whether you're a beginner looking to get started in web development or an experienced developer looking to brush up on your HTML skills, this course has something for you. We hope you'll join us as we dive into the world of HTML and web development!

WHAT IS HTML?

HTML, or Hypertext Markup Language, is the standard markup language for creating web pages. It provides the structure and content for websites, making it an essential skill for any web developer.

Introduction to HTML

HTML is made up of a series of elements, or tags, that are used to mark up the content of a web page. These tags tell the browser how to display the content, whether it's a heading, a paragraph, an image, or a link. HTML tags are usually written in pairs, with an opening tag and a closing tag, and the content of the tag goes in between.

For example, the <h1> tag is used to create a heading, and the <p> tag is used to create a paragraph. To create a link, you can use the <a> tag, and to add an image, you can use the <img> tag.

HTML also has attributes, which provide additional information about the elements. For example, the src attribute specifies the source of an image, and the href attribute specifies the destination of a link.

HTML5

HTML has evolved over the years, and the latest version, HTML5, includes new elements and features that make it easier to create modern, interactive websites. Some of these features include the ability to play audio and video, create graphics with the <canvas> element, and use web components to create reusable chunks of code.

Conclusion

Whether you're a beginner looking to get started in web development or an experienced developer looking to brush up on your HTML skills, learning HTML is an important step in building professional-quality websites.

Exercises

To review these concepts, we will go through a series of exercises designed to test your understanding and apply what you have learned.

What is the purpose of HTML?
How are HTML elements written?
What is the purpose of HTML attributes?
What is the latest version of HTML?
True or false: HTML is used to create interactive websites.

Solutions

What is the purpose of HTML?
The purpose of HTML is to provide the structure and content for websites.

How are HTML elements written?
HTML elements are written in pairs, with an opening tag and a closing tag, and the content of the tag goes in between.

What is the purpose of HTML attributes?
The purpose of HTML attributes is to provide additional information about the elements.

What is the latest version of HTML?
The latest version of HTML is HTML5.

True or false: HTML is used to create interactive websites.
True. HTML5 includes new elements and features that make it easier to create modern, interactive websites.

THE HISTORY OF HTML

HTML, or Hypertext Markup Language, is the standard markup language for creating web pages. It has a long and interesting history that dates back to the early days of the World Wide Web.

The History

HTML was first developed in 1989 by Tim Berners-Lee, a researcher at CERN (the European Organization for Nuclear Research). He was working on a way to share scientific information over the Internet, and he created HTML as a way to structure and format the content of web pages.

The first version of HTML, HTML 1.0, was released in 1991. It was a very basic language, with just a few tags for creating headings, paragraphs, lists, and links.

Over the years, HTML has evolved and grown to include more tags and features. HTML 2.0 was released in 1995, and it introduced new tags for tables, forms, and frames. HTML 3.2, released in 1997, added support for style sheets and other advanced features.

In 2000, HTML 4.01 was released, which added support for XML (Extensible Markup Language) and introduced new tags for multimedia content like audio and video.

Latest Version

The latest version of HTML, HTML5, was released in 2014. It includes new elements and features that make it easier to create modern, interactive websites. Some of these features include the ability to play audio and video, create graphics with the <canvas> element, and use web components to create reusable chunks of code.

Conclusion

Today, HTML is used to create millions of websites, from simple personal blogs to complex e-commerce sites. It has become an essential part of the modern web, and it's a skill that is in high demand among web developers.

Exercises

To review these concepts, we will go through a series of exercises designed to test your understanding and apply what you have learned.

Who developed HTML?
When was the first version of HTML released?
What is the latest version of HTML?
True or false: HTML 4.01 introduced support for XML.

What are some features of HTML5?

Solutions

Who developed HTML?
Tim Berners-Lee developed HTML.

When was the first version of HTML released?
The first version of HTML, HTML 1.0, was released in 1991.

What is the latest version of HTML?
The latest version of HTML is HTML5, which was released in 2014.

True or false: HTML 4.01 introduced support for XML.
True. HTML 4.01 introduced support for XML (Extensible Markup Language).

What are some features of HTML5?
Some features of HTML5 include the ability to play audio and video, create graphics with the <canvas> element, and use web components to create reusable chunks of code.

HOW HTML WORKS

HTML, or Hypertext Markup Language, is a language that is used to create and structure the content of web pages. But how does it actually work?

How Does It Work?

When you visit a website, your web browser sends a request to the server where the website is hosted. The server responds by sending the HTML code for the web page back to your browser.

The browser then reads the HTML code and uses it to render the content of the web page. This process is known as parsing.

HTML is made up of a series of elements, or tags, that are used to mark up the content of a web page. These tags tell the browser how to display the content, whether it's a heading, a paragraph, an image, or a link.

For example, the <h1> tag is used to create a heading, and the <p> tag is used to create a paragraph. To create a link, you can use the <a> tag, and to add an image, you can use the <img> tag.

HTML also has attributes, which provide additional information about the elements. For example, the src attribute specifies the source of an image, and the href attribute specifies the destination of a link.

In addition to HTML, web pages often include other technologies like CSS (Cascading Style Sheets) and JavaScript. CSS is used to apply styles to the content of a web page, and JavaScript is used to add interactivity and dynamic behavior.

Conclusion

Understanding how HTML works is essential for any web developer, as it forms the foundation for building professional-quality websites. With the skills and knowledge you gain in this course, you'll be well on your way to creating your own stunning websites.

Exercises

To review these concepts, we will go through a series of exercises designed to test your understanding and apply what you have learned.

When you visit a website, what sends the HTML code for the web page back to your browser?
What is the process called when the browser reads the HTML code
and uses it to render the content of the web page?
True or false: HTML tags tell the browser how to display the content of a web page.

What is the purpose of HTML attributes?
In addition to HTML, what other technologies are often used on web pages?

Solutions

When you visit a website, what sends the HTML code for the web page back to your browser?
The server sends the HTML code for the web page back to the browser.

**What is the process called when the browser reads the HTML code
and uses it to render the content of the web page?**
The process is called parsing.

True or false: HTML tags tell the browser how to display the content of a web page.
True. HTML tags tell the browser how to display the content of a web page, whether it's a heading, a paragraph, an image, or a link.

What is the purpose of HTML attributes?
The purpose of HTML attributes is to provide additional information about the elements.

In addition to HTML, what other technologies are often used on web pages?
In addition to HTML, web pages often include other technologies like CSS (Cascading Style Sheets) and JavaScript. CSS is used to apply styles to the content of a web page, and JavaScript is used to add interactivity and dynamic behavior.

SETTING UP AN HTML DEVELOPMENT ENVIRONMENT

Before you can start writing HTML code, you need to set up a development environment. A development environment is a software application or set of tools that you use to create and test your code.

Development Environments

There are many different development environments available, and the one you choose will depend on your needs and preferences. Some popular options include:

- Text editors: A text editor is a simple, lightweight program that you can use to write and edit code. Some popular text editors for HTML include Notepad++, Sublime Text, and Atom.
- Integrated development environments (IDEs): An IDE is a more advanced tool that includes features like code completion, debugging, and testing. Some popular IDEs for HTML include Visual Studio Code, NetBeans, and Eclipse.
- Online code editors: An online code editor is a web-based tool that you can use to write and test code right in your browser. Some popular online code editors for HTML include CodePen and JS Bin.

To set up your development environment, you'll need to download and install the software or tool of your choice. Once you have your development environment set up, you'll be ready to start writing and testing your HTML code.

Conclusion

It's important to choose a development environment that is comfortable and efficient for you, as you'll be using it frequently as you learn HTML and build web projects. With the right development environment, you'll be well on your way to creating professional-quality websites.

Exercises

To review these concepts, we will go through a series of exercises designed to test your understanding and apply what you have learned.

What is a development environment?
Name three types of development environments.
Name three popular text editors for HTML.
Name three popular integrated development environments (IDEs) for HTML.
Name two popular online code editors for HTML.

Solutions

What is a development environment?
A development environment is a software application or set of tools that you use to create and test your code.

Name three types of development environments.
Text editors, integrated development environments (IDEs), and online code editors.

Name three popular text editors for HTML.
Notepad++, Sublime Text, and Atom.

Name three popular integrated development environments (IDEs) for HTML.
Visual Studio Code, NetBeans, and Eclipse.

Name two popular online code editors for HTML.
CodePen and JS Bin.

THE STRUCTURE OF AN HTML DOCUMENT

The structure of an HTML document is the foundation of any web page. It determines how the content of the page is organized and displayed, and it's important to understand how it works in order to create professional-quality websites.

In this article, we'll take a deep dive into the structure of an HTML document, including the basic structure, the head and body sections, and the various elements that make up a web page.

Basic Structure of an HTML Document

An HTML document is made up of a series of tags, which are used to mark up the content of the page. These tags tell the browser how to display the content, whether it's a heading, a paragraph, an image, or a link.

Here's the basic structure of an HTML document:

```html
<!DOCTYPE html>
<html>
 <head>
  <!-- The head section goes here -->
 </head>
 <body>
  <!-- The body section goes here -->
 </body>
</html>
```

The <!DOCTYPE html> declaration tells the browser that this is an HTML document. The <html> element is the root element of the document, and it contains all of the other elements.

The <head> element is used to contain information about the document, such as the title, the style sheet, and any meta tags. The <body> element is used to contain the actual content of the page, such as headings, paragraphs, and images.

Head Section

The head section of an HTML document is used to contain information about the document, such as the title, the style sheet, and any meta tags. Here's an example of the head section of an HTML document:

```
<head>
  <title>My Website</title>
  <link rel="stylesheet" href="style.css">
  <meta name="description" content="This is my website">
</head>
```

The <title> element is used to specify the title of the web page, which is displayed in the browser's title bar or tab. The <link> element is used to link to a style sheet, which is a separate file that contains CSS rules that control the appearance of the web page. The <meta> element is used to provide additional information about the document, such as a description or keywords.

Body Section

The body section of an HTML document is used to contain the actual content of the web page. This can include headings, paragraphs, lists, images, links, and any other elements you want to include. Here's an example of the body section of an HTML document:

```
<body>
  <h1>Welcome to My Website</h1>
  <p>This is my website, where I share my thoughts and ideas.</p>
  <ul>
    <li>Home</li>
    <li>About</li>
    <li>Contact</li>
  </ul>
</body>
```

In this example, we have a heading, a paragraph, and an unordered list. The <h1> element is used to create a heading, the <p> element is used to create a paragraph, and the <ul> element is used to create an unordered list. The <li> element is used to create a list item.

Elements and Attributes

HTML elements are usually written in pairs, with an opening tag and a closing tag, and the content of the tag goes in between. For example, the <h1> element is used to create a heading, and it's written like this:

```
<h1>My Heading</h1>
```

HTML also has attributes, which provide additional information about the elements. Attributes are written inside the opening tag, and they consist of a name and a value. For example, the src attribute is used to specify the source of an image, and it's written like this:

```
<img src="image.jpg" alt="My Image">
```

In this example, the src attribute has a value of "image.jpg", and the altattribute has a value of "My Image". The alt attribute is used to provide a text description of the image, which is important for accessibility and search engine optimization.

Block-Level and Inline Elements

HTML elements can be either block-level or inline elements. Block-level elements are elements that create a new block of content, such as headings, paragraphs, and lists. They usually take up the full width of the page and start on a new line.

Inline elements are elements that are used within the flow of text, such as links and images. They don't create a new block of content and don't take up the full width of the page.

Here's an example of block-level and inline elements:

```
<h1>My Heading</h1>
<p>This is a paragraph. <a href="#">This is a link</a> within the paragraph.</p>
```

In this example, the <h1> element is a block-level element, and the <p>element is a block-level element. The <a> element is an inline element, and it's used within the flow of the paragraph.

Conclusion

The structure of an HTML document is the foundation of any web page. It determines how the content of the page is organized and displayed, and it's important to understand how it works in order to create professional-quality websites.

In this article, we looked at the basic structure of an HTML document, including the head and body sections and the various elements that make up a web page. We also explored elements and attributes, and we learned about the difference between block-level and inline elements.

By understanding the structure of an HTML document, you'll have a solid foundation for building web pages that are well-organized, easy to read, and visually appealing. With the skills and knowledge you gain in this course, you'll be well on your way to creating your own stunning websites.

Exercises

To review these concepts, we will go through a series of exercises designed to test your understanding and apply what you have learned.

What is the root element of an HTML document?
What is the purpose of the <head> element in an HTML document?
What is the purpose of the <body> element in an HTML document?
What is the purpose of HTML attributes?
True or false: Inline elements create a new block of content and take up the full width of the page.

Solutions

What is the root element of an HTML document?

The <html> element is the root element of an HTML document.

What is the purpose of the <head> **element in an HTML document?**

The <head> element is used to contain information about the document, such as the title, the style sheet, and any meta tags.

What is the purpose of the <body> **element in an HTML document?**

The <body> element is used to contain the actual content of the web page, such as headings, paragraphs, and images.

What is the purpose of HTML attributes?

HTML attributes provide additional information about the elements. They are written inside the opening tag, and they consist of a name and a value.

True or false: Inline elements create a new block of content and take up the full width of the page.

False. Inline elements are elements that are used within the flow of text, and they don't create a new block of content or take up the full width of the page. Block-level elements are elements that create a new block of content, such as headings, paragraphs, and lists. They usually take up the full width of the page and start on a new line.

HTML TAGS AND ATTRIBUTES

HTML tags and attributes are the building blocks of any web page. They are used to mark up the content of the page and provide additional information about the elements. In this article, we'll take a closer look at HTML tags and attributes, including the different types of tags and the syntax for using them.

Basic HTML Tags

HTML tags are used to mark up the content of a web page. They are written in pairs, with an opening tag and a closing tag, and the content of the tag goes in between. For example, the <h1> tag is used to create a heading, and it's written like this:

```
<h1>My Heading</h1>
```

Here are some basic HTML tags that you'll use frequently:

- <h1> – <h6>: These tags are used to create headings, with <h1> being the largest and <h6> being the smallest.
- <p>: This tag is used to create a paragraph.
-
: This tag is used to create a line break.
- <img>: This tag is used to add an image to a web page.
- <a>: This tag is used to create a link.
- <ul>: This tag is used to create an unordered list (a list with bullet points).
- <ol>: This tag is used to create an ordered list (a numbered list).
- <li>: This tag is used to create a list item.

Here's an example of a basic HTML document using these tags:

```
<h1>My Website</h1>
<p>Welcome to my website. This is where I share my thoughts and ideas.</p>
<p>Here are some things you can do on my website:</p>
<ul>
  <li>Read my blog posts</li>
  <li>Browse my photos</li>
  <li>Contact me</li>
</ul>
```

In this example, we have a heading, two paragraphs, and an unordered list. The <h1> tag is used to create the heading, the <p> tags are used to create the paragraphs, and the <ul> and <li> tags are used to create the list.

HTML Attributes

HTML attributes are used to provide additional information about the elements. They are written inside the opening tag, and they consist of a name and a value. For example, the src attribute is used to specify the source of an image, and it's written like this:

```
<img src="image.jpg" alt="My Image">
```

In this example, the src attribute has a value of "image.jpg", and the altattribute has a value of "My Image". The alt attribute is used to provide a text description of the image, which is important for accessibility and search engine optimization.

Here are some common HTML attributes that you'll use:

- id: This attribute is used to uniquely identify an element. It can be used to apply styles to a specific element or to create links to specific parts of a web page.
- class: This attribute is used to apply a class name to an element, which can be used to apply styles to a group of elements.
- href: This attribute is used to specify the destination of a link. It can be used with the <a> tag to create a link to another web page or to a specific part of the same page.
- src: This attribute is used to specify the source of an image. It can be used with the <img> tag to add an image to a web page.
- alt: This attribute is used to provide a text description of an image. It's important for accessibility and search engine optimization, and it's used with the <img> tag.

Here's an example of an HTML document using these attributes:

```
<h1 id="title">My Website</h1>
<p class="intro">Welcome to my website. This is where I share my thoughts and ideas.</p>
<p>Here are some things you can do on my website:</p>
<ul>
  <li><a href="/blog">Read my blog posts</a></li>
  <li><a href="/photos">Browse my photos</a></li>
  <li><a href="/contact">Contact me</a></li>
</ul>
<img src="profile.jpg" alt="My profile picture">
```

In this example, we have an id attribute on the <h1> element, a classattribute on the <p> element, and href attributes on the <a> elements. We also have a src attribute on the <img> element and an alt attribute to provide a text description of the image.

HTML5 Semantic Elements

HTML5 introduced a new set of semantic elements that provide additional meaning to the content of a web page. These elements make it easier for search engines and screen readers to understand the structure and content of a web page, and they can also make it easier for developers to style and organize the content.

Here are some common HTML5 semantic elements:

- <header>: This element is used to contain the header of a web page or section. It can include a logo, a navigation menu, and other elements.
- <nav>: This element is used to contain the navigation links for a web page or section.
- <main>: This element is used to contain the main content of a web page. It should only be used once per page.
- <article>: This element is used to contain a standalone piece of content, such as a blog post or a news article.
- <section>: This element is used to contain a group of related content, such as a chapter or a section of a document.
- <aside>: This element is used to contain content that is related to the main content, but not essential to the understanding of it. It could be a sidebar, a related links section, or other elements.
- <footer>: This element is used to contain the footer of a web page or section. It can include a copyright notice, a list of links, and other elements.

Here's an example of an HTML document using these elements:

```html
<header>
<h1>My Website</h1>
<nav>
<ul>
<li><a href="/">Home</a></li>
<li><a href="/about">About</a></li>
<li><a href="/blog">Blog</a></li>
<li><a href="/contact">Contact</a></li>
</ul>
</nav>
</header>
<main>
<article>
<h2>My Latest Blog Post</h2>
<p>Lorem ipsum dolor sit amet, consectetur adipiscing elit. Mauris id ornare leo. Ut tincidunt lacus sed justo placerat, sed aliquam libero dictum. Pellentesque habitant morbi tristique senectus et netus et malesuada fames ac turpis egestas. Aliquam id dolor mollis, suscipit lacus in, pharetis lacus. Proin fermentum leo id sem efficitur, quis dictum nibh efficitur. Aliquam consectetur pretium est, a convallis erat cursus vel. Morbi vel bibendum velit. Suspendisse placerat turpis in diam porttitor pretium. Maecenas id turpis eu nisi efficitur pharetra in at diam.</p>
</article>
<section>
<h2>About Me</h2>
```

```
    <p>Lorem ipsum dolor sit amet, consectetur adipiscing elit. Mauris id ornare leo. Ut tincidunt lacus
sed justo placerat, sed aliquam libero dictum. Pellentesque habitant morbi tristique senectus et netus
et malesuada fames ac turpis egestas. Aliquam id dolor mollis, suscipit lacus in, pharetra lacus. Proin
fermentum leo id sem efficitur, quis dictum nibh efficitur. Aliquam consectetur pretium est, a convallis
erat cursus vel. Morbi vel bibendum velit. Suspendisse placerat turpis in diam porttitor pretium.
Maecenas id turpis eu nisi efficitur pharetra in at diam.</p>
    </section>
    </main>
    <aside>
    <h3>Related Links</h3>
    <ul>
      <li><a href="#">Link 1</a></li>
      <li><a href="#">Link 2</a></li>
      <li><a href="#">Link 3</a></li>
    </ul>
    </aside>
    <footer>
    <p>Copyright 2022 My Website</p>
    </footer>
```

In this example, we have a header with a logo and a navigation menu, a main section with an article and a section, an aside with related links, and a footer with a copyright notice. The semantic elements make it easier to understand the structure and content of the web page, and they can also make it easier to style and organize the content.

Conclusion

HTML tags and attributes are the building blocks of any web page. They are used to mark up the content of the page and provide additional information about the elements. Understanding how to use tags and attributes is essential for creating well-organized, professional-quality web pages. With the skills and knowledge you gain in this course, you'll be well on your way to creating your own stunning websites.

Exercises

To review these concepts, we will go through a series of exercises designed to test your understanding and apply what you have learned.

What is the purpose of HTML tags?
What is the syntax for using an HTML attribute?
What is the purpose of the <main> **element in HTML5?**
What is the purpose of the class **attribute in HTML?**
True or false: The <header> **element can only be used once per web page.**

Solutions

What is the purpose of HTML tags?

HTML tags are used to mark up the content of a web page. They are written in pairs, with an opening tag and a closing tag, and the content of the tag goes in between.

What is the syntax for using an HTML attribute?

HTML attributes are written inside the opening tag, and they consist of a name and a value. For example: <tag attribute="value">.

What is the purpose of the <main> **element in HTML5?**

The <main> element is used to contain the main content of a web page. It should only be used once per page.

What is the purpose of the class **attribute in HTML?**

The class attribute is used to apply a class name to an element, which can be used to apply styles to a group of elements.

True or false: The <header> **element can only be used once per web page.**

False. The <header> element can be used multiple times per web page to contain different header sections. It's common to use a separate <header> element for the main header of a web page and for the headers of individual sections or articles.

CREATING HEADINGS AND PARAGRAPHS

Headings and paragraphs are essential elements of any web page. They are used to organize and structure the content of the page, and they make it easier for users to read and understand the information. In this article, we'll take a closer look at how to create headings and paragraphs in HTML.

Creating Headings

HTML provides six levels of headings, from <h1> to <h6>, with <h1> being the largest and <h6> being the smallest. Headings are important for outlining the structure and hierarchy of the content on a web page, and they should be used to indicate the main points and sections of the page.

Here's an example of how to create headings in HTML:

```
<h1>My Website</h1>
<h2>About Me</h2>
<h3>My Hobbies</h3>
<h4>Travel</h4>
<h5>Food</h5>
<h6>Photography</h6>
```

In this example, we have created six headings at different levels, with the <h1> heading being the main heading of the page and the <h2> to <h6>headings being subheadings.

It's important to use headings appropriately and in a logical order. The main heading of the page should be an <h1> heading, and the subheadings should be <h2> headings or lower. Avoid skipping heading levels or using multiple <h1> headings on the same page.

Creating Paragraphs

Paragraphs are used to contain blocks of text on a web page. They are created with the ` <p> ` tag, and the text goes in between the opening and closing tags.

Here's an example of how to create a paragraph in HTML:

```
<p>Lorem ipsum dolor sit amet, consectetur adipiscing elit. Mauris id ornare leo. Ut tincidunt lacus sed justo placerat, sed aliquam libero dictum.</p>
```

In this example, we have created a paragraph containing a block of placeholder text. The <p> tag surrounds the text, and it indicates that it is a paragraph.

You can also use line breaks to separate blocks of text within a paragraph. The <br> tag creates a line break, and it can be used to create a new line within a paragraph.

```
<p>Lorem ipsum dolor sit amet, consectetur adipiscing elit. Mauris id ornare leo.<br>
Ut tincidunt lacus sed justo placerat, sed aliquam libero dictum.</p>
```

In this example, we have used a line break to create a new line within the paragraph.

Formatting Text

HTML also provides a number of tags for formatting text, such as bold, italic, and underline. These tags can be used to highlight important words or phrases, or to add emphasis to the content.

Here's an example of how to use text formatting tags in HTML:

```
<p>This is an <strong>important</strong> paragraph.</p>
<p>This paragraph has some <em>emphasis</em> on certain words.</p>
<p>This paragraph has a <u>word</u> underlined.</p>
```

In this example, we have used the <strong> tag to make the word "important" bold, the <em> tag to italicize the word "emphasis", and the <u>tag to underline the word "word".

There are also tags for creating small and large text, as well as for creating subscript and superscript text. Here are some examples:

```
<p>This is <small>small</small> text.</p>
<p>This is <big>big</big> text.</p>
<p>This is a <sub>subscript</sub> text.</p>
<p>This is a <sup>superscript</sup> text.</p>
```

It's important to use text formatting tags appropriately and sparingly. Overuse of text formatting can make the content hard to read and can diminish the effectiveness of the formatting.

Conclusion

Headings and paragraphs are essential elements of any web page, and they are used to organize and structure the content. With the skills and knowledge you gain in this course, you'll be able to create professional-quality web pages that are easy to read and understand.

Exercises

To review these concepts, we will go through a series of exercises designed to test your understanding and apply what you have learned.

How many levels of headings are there in HTML?
What is the purpose of the <p> tag in HTML?
How can you create a line break within a paragraph in HTML?

How can you italicize a word or phrase in HTML?
True or false: It's a good idea to use text formatting tags excessively in HTML.

Solutions

How many levels of headings are there in HTML?
There are six levels of headings in HTML, from <h1> to <h6>, with <h1>being the largest and <h6> being the smallest.

What is the purpose of the <p> tag in HTML?
The <p> tag is used to create a paragraph in HTML. It surrounds the text of the paragraph and indicates that it is a paragraph.

How can you create a line break within a paragraph in HTML?
You can use the <br> tag to create a line break within a paragraph in HTML.

How can you italicize a word or phrase in HTML?
You can use the <em> tag to italicize a word or phrase in HTML.

True or false: It's a good idea to use text formatting tags excessively in HTML.
False. It's important to use text formatting tags appropriately and sparingly. Overuse of text formatting can make the content hard to read and can diminish the effectiveness of the formatting.

ADDING IMAGES AND LINKS

Images and links are essential elements of any web page. They add visual interest and enhance the user experience, and they allow users to navigate between different pages and resources on the web. In this article, we'll take a closer look at how to add images and links in HTML.

Adding Images

HTML provides the <img> tag for adding images to web pages. The <img>tag is a self-closing tag, meaning it doesn't have a closing tag, and it requires the src attribute to specify the source of the image.

Here's an example of how to add an image to a web page in HTML:

```
<img src="/images/my-image.jpg" alt="My Image">
```

In this example, we have added an image to the web page with the <img>tag. The src attribute specifies the source of the image, which is the file path to the image. The alt attribute is used to provide a text alternative for the image, which is important for accessibility and for search engines.

The <img> tag also supports a number of other attributes, such as widthand height for specifying the size of the image, and title for providing a tooltip when the image is hovered over.

```
<img src="/images/my-image.jpg" alt="My Image" width="200" height="200" title="My Image">
```

In this example, we have added the width and height attributes to specify the size of the image, and the title attribute to provide a tooltip when the image is hovered over.

It's important to use descriptive, relevant filenames for your images, and to specify the correct file path in the src attribute. You should also optimize your images for web by compressing them and sizing them appropriately.

Adding Links

HTML provides the <a> tag for creating links to other web pages or resources. The <a> tag is an inline element that requires the href attribute to specify the destination of the link.

Here's an example of how to add a link to a web page in HTML:

```
<a href="https://www.example.com">Example</a>
```

In this example, we have added a link to the web page with the <a> tag. The href attribute specifies the destination of the link, which is the URL of the page. The text between the opening and closing tags is the text of the link.

You can also use the target attribute to specify how the link should be opened. For example, you can use _blank to open the link in a new window or tab.

```
<a href="https://www.example.com" target="_blank">Example</a>
```

In this example, we have added the target attribute to specify that the link should be opened in a new window or tab.

You can also use the rel attribute to specify the relationship between the current page and the linked page. For example, you can use nofollow to indicate that the link should not be followed by search engines.

```
<a href="https://www.example.com" rel="nofollow">Example</a>
```

In this example, we have added the rel attribute to indicate that the link should not be followed by search engines.

It's important to use descriptive, relevant anchor text for your links, and to specify the correct destination in the href attribute. You should also avoid using broken or irrelevant links, as they can negatively impact the user experience and the credibility of your site.

Conclusion

Images and links are important elements of any web page, and they add visual interest and enhance the user experience. With the skills and knowledge you gain in this course, you'll be able to add professional-quality images and links to your web pages.

Exercises

To review these concepts, we will go through a series of exercises designed to test your understanding and apply what you have learned.

What is the purpose of the src **attribute in the** <img> **tag in HTML?**
What is the purpose of the alt **attribute in the** <img> **tag in HTML?**
What is the purpose of the href **attribute in the** <a> **tag in HTML?**
What is the purpose of the target **attribute in the** <a> **tag in HTML?**
What is the purpose of the rel **attribute in the** <a> **tag in HTML?**

Solutions

What is the purpose of the src **attribute in the** <img> **tag in HTML?**
The src attribute in the <img> tag is used to specify the source of the image. It is the file path to the image.

What is the purpose of the alt **attribute in the** <img> **tag in HTML?**
The alt attribute in the <img> tag is used to provide a text alternative for the image. It is important for accessibility and for search engines.

What is the purpose of the href **attribute in the** <a> **tag in HTML?**

The href attribute in the <a> tag is used to specify the destination of the link. It is the URL of the page.

What is the purpose of the target **attribute in the** <a> **tag in HTML?**

The target attribute in the <a> tag is used to specify how the link should be opened. For example, you can use _blank to open the link in a new window or tab.

What is the purpose of the rel **attribute in the** <a> **tag in HTML?**

The rel attribute in the <a> tag is used to specify the relationship between the current page and the linked page. For example, you can use nofollow to indicate that the link should not be followed by search engines.

USING DIV AND SPAN ELEMENTS

Div and span elements are essential elements of any web page. They are used to group and style content on the page, and they provide a way to apply styles to specific areas of the page. In this article, we'll take a closer look at how to use div and span elements in HTML.

Using Div Elements

The <div> element is a block-level element that is used to group and style content on a web page. It can contain any type of content, including headings, paragraphs, lists, and other elements. The <div> element is often used as a container for other elements, and it can be styled with CSS to create a wide range of layouts and designs.

Here's an example of how to use a div element in HTML:

```
<div>
 <h2>My Website</h2>
 <p>Welcome to my website!</p>
</div>
```

In this example, we have used a div element to group a heading and a paragraph. The <h2> and <p> elements are nested within the <div>element, and they are styled and positioned as a unit.

You can also use the id and class attributes to apply styles to div elements. The id attribute is used to uniquely identify an element on the page, and the class attribute is used to apply styles to multiple elements on the page.

```
<div id="header" class="container">
 <h2>My Website</h2>
 <p>Welcome to my website!</p>
</div>
```

In this example, we have added the id and class attributes to the div element. The id attribute uniquely identifies the element as the header, and the class attribute applies the style of a container to the element.

Using Span Elements

The <span> element is an inline element that is used to group and style content within a block of text. It can contain any type of inline content, such as words or phrases. The <span> element is often used to apply styles to specific parts of a block of text, and it can be styled with CSS to create a wide range of effects.

Here's an example of how to use a span element in HTML:

```
<p>Welcome to <span>my website</span>!</p>
```

In this example, we have used a span element to group the phrase "my website" within a paragraph. The <span> element is nested within the <p>element, and it can be styled to change the appearance of the phrase within the paragraph.

Like div elements, span elements can also be styled using the id and class attributes.

```
<p>Welcome to <span id="website-name" class="highlight">my website</span>!</p>
```

In this example, we have added the id and class attributes to the span element. The id attribute uniquely identifies the element as the website name, and the class attribute applies the style of a highlight to the element.

Conclusion

Div and span elements are essential elements of any web page, and they are used to group and style content on the page. With the skills and knowledge you gain in this course, you'll be able to use div and span elements to create professional-quality web pages that are visually appealing and easy to read.

Exercises

To review these concepts, we will go through a series of exercises designed to test your understanding and apply what you have learned.

True or false: The <div> **element is an inline element.**
What type of content can be contained within a <div>**element?**
What is the purpose of the id **attribute in an HTML element?**
True or false: The <span> **element is a block-level element.**
What type of content can be contained within a <span>**element?**

Solutions

True or false: The <div> **element is an inline element.**
False. The <div> element is a block-level element.

What type of content can be contained within a <div>**element?**
A <div> element can contain any type of content, including headings, paragraphs, lists, and other elements.

What is the purpose of the id **attribute in an HTML element?**
The id attribute is used to uniquely identify an element on the page.

True or false: The <span> **element is a block-level element.**
False. The <span> element is an inline element.

What type of content can be contained within a <span>**element?**
A <span> element can contain any type of inline content, such as words or phrases.

APPLYING STYLES WITH CSS

CSS (Cascading Style Sheets) is a style sheet language that is used to describe the look and formatting of a document written in HTML. It allows you to apply styles, such as fonts, colors, and layouts, to your web pages in a consistent and efficient manner. In this article, we'll take a closer look at how to apply styles with CSS.

Getting Started with CSS

There are three ways to apply CSS to an HTML document: inline, internal, and external.

Inline CSS is applied directly to an HTML element using the styleattribute. It is best used for small, specific styles that apply to a single element.

Here's an example of how to use inline CSS in HTML:

```
<p style="color: red; font-size: 20px;">
This is a paragraph with inline CSS.</p>
```

In this example, we have applied the style of a red font color and a font size of 20 pixels to the paragraph using the style attribute.

Internal CSS is applied to an HTML document using a <style> element in the <head> of the document. It is best used for styles that apply to multiple elements throughout the document.

Here's an example of how to use internal CSS in HTML:

```
<head>
  <style>
    p {
      color: red;
      font-size: 20px;
    }
  </style>
</head>
```

In this example, we have applied the style of a red font color and a font size of 20 pixels to all paragraphs in the document using the <style>element.

External CSS is applied to an HTML document using a separate CSS file. It is best used for styles that apply to multiple pages or a large website.

Here's an example of how to use external CSS in HTML:

```
<head>
<link rel="stylesheet" href="/css/style.css">
</head>
```

In this example, we have linked to an external CSS file using the <link>element in the <head> of the document. The rel attribute specifies the relationship between the HTML document and the CSS file, and the hrefattribute specifies the location of the CSS file.

CSS Syntax

CSS has a simple syntax that consists of selectors, properties, and values.

Selectors are used to select the elements on the page that you want to style. There are three types of selectors: element, class, and id.

Element selectors are used to apply styles to all instances of a particular element. They are denoted by the element name, such as p for paragraphs or h1 for headings.

Class selectors are used to apply styles to a group of elements that share a common class. They are denoted by a period followed by the class name, such as .highlight for highlighted elements.

Id selectors are used to apply styles to a specific element on the page. They are denoted by a pound sign followed by the id name, such

as #header for the header element.

Properties are the characteristics of an element that you want to style. They are denoted by a property name, such as color, font-size, or background-color.

Values are the specific values that you want to apply to a property. They are denoted by a value, such as red, 20px, or #fff.

Here's an example of a CSS rule:

```
p {
color: red;
font-size: 20px;
}
```

In this example, we have selected all paragraphs using the element selector p, and we have applied the properties of a red font color and a font size of 20 pixels using the values red and 20px.

CSS Inheritance

CSS inheritance is a way for child elements to inherit the styles of their parent elements. This means that if you apply a style to a parent element, it will be applied to all of its child elements as well.

For example, if you apply the style of a red font color to a div element, all of the elements within the div will also have a red font color.

```
<div style="color: red;">
  <p>This is a paragraph with a red font color.</p>
  <h2>This is a heading with a red font color.</h2>
</div>
```

In this example, both the paragraph and the heading have inherited the style of a red font color from the div element.

You can also use the inherit value to explicitly inherit a style from a parent element.

```
<div style="color: red;">
  <p style="color: inherit;">
  This is a paragraph with a red font color.</p>
</div>
```

In this example, the paragraph has explicitly inherited the style of a red font color from the div element.

Conclusion

CSS is a powerful style sheet language that allows you to apply styles to your web pages in a consistent and efficient manner. With the skills and knowledge you gain in this course, you'll be able to use CSS to create professional-quality web pages that are visually appealing and easy to read.

Exercises

To review these concepts, we will go through a series of exercises designed to test your understanding and apply what you have learned.

How do you apply inline CSS to an HTML element?
How do you apply internal CSS to an HTML document?
How do you apply external CSS to an HTML document?
What is a property in CSS?
What is a value in CSS?

Solutions

How do you apply inline CSS to an HTML element?
To apply inline CSS to an HTML element, use the style attribute and specify the properties and values that you want to apply. For example:

```
<p style="color: red; font-size: 20px;">
This is a paragraph with inline CSS.</p>
```

How do you apply internal CSS to an HTML document?

To apply internal CSS to an HTML document, use the <style> element in the <head> of the document and specify the selectors, properties, and values that you want to apply. For example:

```
<head>
<style>
p {
  color: red;
  font-size: 20px;
}
</style>
</head>
```

How do you apply external CSS to an HTML document?

To apply external CSS to an HTML document, use the <link> element in the <head> of the document and specify the location of the CSS file using the href attribute. For example:

```
<head>
<link rel="stylesheet" href="/css/style.css">
</head>
```

What is a property in CSS?

A property in CSS is a characteristic of an element that you want to style. It is denoted by a property name, such as color, font-size, or background-color.

What is a value in CSS?

A value in CSS is a specific value that you want to apply to a property. It is denoted by a value, such as red, 20px, or #fff.

CREATING LISTS AND TABLES

Lists and tables are essential elements of any web page, and they are used to organize and present data in a clear and concise manner. In this article, we'll take a closer look at how to create lists and tables in HTML.

Creating Lists

There are three types of lists in HTML: ordered lists, unordered lists, and definition lists.

Ordered lists are used to display a list of items in a specific order, and they are denoted by the <ol> element. Each item in the list is represented by a <li> element.

Here's an example of how to create an ordered list in HTML:

```
<ol>
  <li>Item 1</li>
  <li>Item 2</li>
  <li>Item 3</li>
</ol>
```

In this example, we have created an ordered list using the <ol> element, and we have added three items to the list using the <li> element. The list will be displayed with numbers corresponding to the order of the items.

Unordered lists are used to display a list of items in no particular order, and they are denoted by the <ul> element. Each item in the list is represented by a <li> element.

Here's an example of how to create an unordered list in HTML:

```
<ul>
  <li>Item 1</li>
  <li>Item 2</li>
  <li>Item 3</li>
</ul>
```

In this example, we have created an unordered list using the <ul> element, and we have added three items to the list using the <li> element. The list will be displayed with bullet points corresponding to the items.

Definition lists are used to display a list of terms and their definitions, and they are denoted by the <dl> element. Each term is represented by a <dt>element, and each definition is represented by a <dd> element.

Here's an example of how to create a definition list in HTML:

```
<dl>
<dt>Term 1</dt>
<dd>Definition 1</dd>
<dt>Term 2</dt>
<dd>Definition 2</dd>
<dt>Term 3</dt>
<dd>Definition 3</dd>
</dl>
```

Creating Tables

Tables are used to display data in rows and columns, and they are denoted by the <table> element.

To create a table in HTML, you need to use the following elements:

- <table>: the main container for the table
- <tr>: a row in the table
- <th>: a table header cell
- <td>: a table data cell

Here's an example of how to create a basic table in HTML:

```
<table>
<tr>
<th>Name</th>
<th>Age</th>
<th>Gender</th>
</tr>
<tr>
<td>John</td>
<td>30</td>
<td>Male</td>
</tr>
<tr>
<td>Jane</td>
<td>25</td>
<td>Female</td>
```

```
</tr>
```

```
</table>
```

In this example, we have created a table using the <table> element, and we have added three rows to the table using the <tr> element. Each row has three cells, which are defined using the <th> and <td> elements. The <th> element is used for the table header cells, and the <td> element is used for the table data cells.

Styling Tables

You can use CSS to style your tables and make them more visually appealing. Some common properties that you can use to style tables include:

- border: adds a border to the table
- border-collapse: specifies whether the table borders should be collapsed into a single border or separated into individual borders
- width: specifies the width of the table
- height: specifies the height of the table

Here's an example of how to use CSS to style a table:

```css
table {
  border: 1px solid #ccc;
  border-collapse: collapse;
  width: 100%;
  height: 200px;
}
```

In this example, we have applied the styles of a 1 pixel solid border with a color of #ccc, collapsed borders, a width of 100%, and a height of 200 pixels to the table using the border, border-collapse, width, and heightproperties.

Conclusion

Lists and tables are essential elements of any web page, and they are used to organize and present data in a clear and concise manner. With the skills and knowledge you gain in this course, you'll be able to create professional-quality lists and tables that are easy to read and understand. You can also use CSS to style your lists and tables and make them more visually appealing.

Exercises

To review these concepts, we will go through a series of exercises designed to test your understanding and apply what you have learned.

How do you create an ordered list in HTML?
How do you create an unordered list in HTML?
How do you create a definition list in HTML?
What elements do you need to use to create a table in HTML?

What are some common CSS properties that you can use to style tables?

Solutions

How do you create an ordered list in HTML?

To create an ordered list in HTML, use the <ol> element and add each item to the list using the <li> element. For example:

```
<ol>
<li>Item 1</li>
<li>Item 2</li>
<li>Item 3</li>
</ol>
```

How do you create an unordered list in HTML?

To create an unordered list in HTML, use the <ul> element and add each item to the list using the <li> element. For example:

```
<ul>
<li>Item 1</li>
<li>Item 2</li>
<li>Item 3</li>
</ul>
```

How do you create a definition list in HTML?

To create a definition list in HTML, use the <dl> element and add each term and definition using the <dt> and <dd> elements. For example:

```
<dl>
<dt>Term 1</dt>
<dd>Definition 1</dd>
<dt>Term 2</dt>
<dd>Definition 2</dd>
<dt>Term 3</dt>
<dd>Definition 3</dd>
</dl>
```

What elements do you need to use to create a table in HTML?

To create a table in HTML, you need to use the <table> element for the main container, the <tr> element for each row, the <th> element for the table header cells, and the <td> element for the table data cells.

What are some common CSS properties that you can use to style tables?

Some common CSS properties that you can use to style tables include border, border-collapse, width, and height.

USING HTML LAYOUT TAGS

HTML layout tags are essential elements of any web page, and they are used to structure and organize the content on a page. In this article, we'll take a closer look at how to use HTML layout tags to create a well-designed and visually appealing web page.

HTML Headings

Headings are used to denote the importance of text, and they are denoted by the <h1>, <h2>, <h3>, <h4>, <h5>, and <h6> elements. The <h1> element represents the most important heading, and the <h6> element represents the least important heading.

Here's an example of how to use headings in HTML:

```
<h1>This is a level 1 heading</h1>
<h2>This is a level 2 heading</h2>
<h3>This is a level 3 heading</h3>
<h4>This is a level 4 heading</h4>
<h5>This is a level 5 heading</h5>
<h6>This is a level 6 heading</h6>
```

In this example, we have used headings of various levels to denote the importance of the text.

HTML Paragraphs

Paragraphs are used to group related text, and they are denoted by the <p> element.

Here's an example of how to use paragraphs in HTML:

```
<p>This is the first paragraph.</p>
<p>This is the second paragraph.</p>
<p>This is the third paragraph.</p>
```

In this example, we have created three paragraphs using the <p> element.

HTML Divisions

Divisions are used to group related content into logical sections, and they are denoted by the <div> element.

Here's an example of how to use divisions in HTML:

```
<div>
    <p>This is the first paragraph in the division.</p>
    <p>This is the second paragraph in the division.</p>
</div>
<div>
    <p>
    <p>This is the second paragraph in the second division.</p>
</div>
```

In this example, we have created two divisions using the <div> element, and we have added paragraphs to each division.

HTML Spans

Spans are used to apply styles to inline elements, and they are denoted by the <span> element.

Here's an example of how to use spans in HTML:

```
<p>This is a <span style="color: red;">
red</span> word.</p>
```

In this example, we have used a span to apply the color red to the word "red".

HTML Anchors

Anchors are used to create hyperlinks, and they are denoted by the <a>element.

Here's an example of how to use anchors in HTML:

```
<a href="https://www.example.com">
This is a link to example.com</a>
```

In this example, we have used an anchor to create a hyperlink to the example.com website.

HTML Images

Images are used to display graphics on a web page, and they are denoted by the <img> element.

Here's an example of how to use images in HTML:

```
<img src="/path/to/image.jpg" alt="Alt text">
```

In this example, we have used the <img> element to display an image located at the specified path, and we have added alt text for accessibility purposes.

Conclusion

HTML layout tags are essential elements of any web page, and they are used to structure and organize the content on a page. With the skills and knowledge you gain in this course, you'll be able to create professional-quality web pages that are easy to read and navigate.

Exercises

To review these concepts, we will go through a series of exercises designed to test your understanding and apply what you have learned.

What element is used to denote headings in HTML?
What element is used to group related text into paragraphs in HTML?
What element is used to group related content into logical sections in HTML?
What element is used to apply styles to inline elements in HTML?
What element is used to create hyperlinks in HTML?

Solutions

What element is used to denote headings in HTML?
Solution: The <h1>, <h2>, <h3>, <h4>, <h5>, <h6> elements are used to denote headings in HTML.

What element is used to group related text into paragraphs in HTML?
The <p> element is used to group related text into paragraphs in HTML.

What element is used to group related content into logical sections in HTML?
The <div> element is used to group related content into logical sections in HTML.

What element is used to apply styles to inline elements in HTML?
The <span> element is used to apply styles to inline elements in HTML.

What element is used to create hyperlinks in HTML?
The <a> element is used to create hyperlinks in HTML.

CREATING INPUT FIELDS AND BUTTONS

Input fields and buttons are essential elements of any web page, and they are used to allow users to interact with the page and provide input. In this article, we'll take a closer look at how to create input fields and buttons in HTML.

HTML Input Fields

Input fields are used to allow users to enter data, and they are denoted by the <input> element.

There are various types of input fields that you can use in HTML, including text fields, password fields, radio buttons, checkboxes, and more.

Here's an example of how to create a text field in HTML:

```
<input type="text" placeholder="Enter your name">
```

In this example, we have created a text field using the <input> element and the type attribute set to "text". We have also added a placeholder attribute to provide a hint to the user.

Here's an example of how to create a password field in HTML:

```
<input type="password"
placeholder="Enter your password">
```

In this example, we have created a password field using the <input>element and the type attribute set to "password". We have also added a placeholder attribute to provide a hint to the user.

HTML Buttons

Buttons are used to allow users to interact with the page and trigger actions, and they are denoted by the <button> element.

Here's an example of how to create a button in HTML:

```
<button>Click me</button>
```

In this example, we have created a button using the <button> element and added text to the button using the inner HTML.

Styling Input Fields and Buttons

You can use CSS to style your input fields and buttons and make them more visually appealing. Some common properties that you can use to style input fields and buttons include:

- color: specifies the color of the text
- background-color: specifies the background color of the element
- border: adds a border to the element
- font-size: specifies the font size of the text

Here's an example of how to use CSS to style an input field:

```
input[type="text"] {
  color: #000;
  background-color: #fff;
  border: 1px solid #ccc;
  font-size: 16px;
}
```

In this example, we have applied the styles of a black text color, a white background color, a 1 pixel solid border with a color of #ccc, and a font size of 16 pixels to the input field using the color, background-color, border, and font-size properties.

Here's an example of how to use CSS to style a button:

```
button {
  color: #fff;
  background-color: #000;
  border: none;
  font-size: 16px;
}
```

In this example, we have applied the styles of a white text color, a black background color, no border, and a font size of 16 pixels to the button using the color, background-color, border, and font-size properties.

Conclusion

Input fields and buttons are essential elements of any web page, and they allow users to interact with the page and provide input. With the skills and knowledge you gain in this course, you'll be able to create professional-quality input fields and buttons that are easy to use and visually appealing.

Exercises

To review these concepts, we will go through a series of exercises designed to test your understanding and apply what you have learned.

What element is used to create input fields in HTML?
What attribute is used to specify the type of input field in HTML?

What element is used to create buttons in HTML?
What property is used to specify the color of the text in CSS?
What property is used to specify the background color of an element in CSS?

Solutions

What element is used to create input fields in HTML?

The <input> element is used to create input fields in HTML.

What attribute is used to specify the type of input field in HTML?

The type attribute is used to specify the type of input field in HTML.

What element is used to create buttons in HTML?

The <button> element is used to create buttons in HTML.

What property is used to specify the color of the text in CSS?

The color property is used to specify the color of the text in CSS.

What property is used to specify the background color of an element in CSS?

The background-color property is used to specify the background color of an element in CSS.

HANDLING USER INPUT WITH FORM HANDLING TECHNIQUES

Form handling techniques are essential for any web page that requires user input, and they allow you to process and validate user input before it is submitted. In this article, we'll take a closer look at how to handle user input with form handling techniques in HTML.

HTML Forms

Forms are used to collect user input, and they are denoted by the <form>element.

Here's an example of how to create a form in HTML:

```
<form action="/process-form.php" method="post">
 <input type="text" name="username" placeholder="Enter your username">
 <input type="password" name="password" placeholder="Enter your password">
 <button type="submit">Log in</button>
</form>
```

In this example, we have created a form using the <form> element and added two input fields and a button. We have also specified the action attribute with the URL of the script that will process the form, and the method attribute with the HTTP method to use when submitting the form.

Form Validation

Form validation is the process of checking that user input is valid before it is submitted.

There are various techniques that you can use to validate user input in HTML, including client-side and server-side validation.

Client-side validation is performed by the web browser, and it is generally faster and more efficient than server-side validation. However, it is also less secure, as users can disable or bypass client-side validation.

Server-side validation is performed by the web server, and it is generally slower and less efficient than client-side validation. However, it is also more secure, as users cannot disable or bypass server-side validation.

HTML provides various attributes that you can use to validate user input, including:

- required: specifies that the input field is required
- pattern: specifies a regular expression that the input field must match
- min and max: specify the minimum and maximum values that the input field can have

Here's an example of how to use the required attribute to validate user input in HTML:

```
<input type="text" name="username"
placeholder="Enter your username" required>
```

In this example, we have added the required attribute to the input field, which specifies that the input field is required and that the user must enter a value.

Here's an example of how to use the pattern attribute to validate user input in HTML:

```
<input type="text" name="email"
placeholder="Enter your email"
pattern="[a-z0-9._%+-]+@[a-z0-9.-]+\.[a-z]{2,}$">
```

In this example, we have added the pattern attribute to the input field, which specifies a regular expression that the input field must match. In this case, the regular expression specifies that the input must be a valid email address.

Here's an example of how to use the min and max attributes to validate user input in HTML:

```
<input type="number" name="age"
placeholder="Enter your age" min="18" max="120">
```

In this example, we have added the min and max attributes to the input field, which specify the minimum and maximum values that the input field can have. In this case, the input field can only accept values between 18 and 120.

Form Processing

Form processing is the process of handling the user input after it has been submitted.

There are various techniques that you can use to process user input in HTML, including client-side and server-side processing.

Client-side processing is performed by the web browser, and it is generally faster and more efficient than server-side processing. However, it is also less secure, as users can disable or bypass client-side processing.

Server-side processing is performed by the web server, and it is generally slower and less efficient than client-side processing. However, it is also more secure, as users cannot disable or bypass server-side processing.

HTML provides various methods that you can use to process user input, including:

- GET: sends the data in the form as a query string in the URL
- POST: sends the data in the form as a request body

Here's an example of how to use the POST method to process user input in HTML:

```
<form action="/process-form.php" method="post">
  <input type="text" name="username" placeholder="Enter your username">
  <input type="password" name="password" placeholder="Enter your password">
  <button type="submit">Log in</button>
</form>
```

In this example, we have specified the POST method in the form using the method attribute, and we have specified the URL of the script that will process the form using the action attribute. When the user submits the form, the data will be sent as a request body to the specified URL.

Conclusion

Form handling techniques are essential for any web page that requires user input, and they allow you to process and validate user input before it is submitted. With the skills and knowledge you gain in this course, you'll be able to create professional-quality forms that are easy to use and secure.

Exercises

To review these concepts, we will go through a series of exercises designed to test your understanding and apply what you have learned.

What element is used to create forms in HTML?
What attribute is used to specify the HTTP method to use when submitting a form in HTML?
What attribute is used to specify the URL of the script that will process the form in HTML?
What attribute is used to specify that an input field is required in HTML?
What attribute is used to specify a regular expression that an input field must match in HTML?

Solutions

What element is used to create forms in HTML?
The <form> element is used to create forms in HTML.

What attribute is used to specify the HTTP method to use when submitting a form in HTML?
The method attribute is used to specify the HTTP method to use when submitting a form in HTML.

What attribute is used to specify the URL of the script that will process the form in HTML?
The action attribute is used to specify the URL of the script that will process the form in HTML.

What attribute is used to specify that an input field is required in HTML?
The required attribute is used to specify that an input field is required in HTML.

What attribute is used to specify a regular expression that an input field must match in HTML?
The pattern attribute is used to specify a regular expression that an input field must match in HTML.

VALIDATING AND PROCESSING FORM DATA

Validating and processing form data is an essential part of any web page that requires user input, and it allows you to ensure that user input is valid and properly handled before it is submitted. In this article, we'll take a closer look at how to validate and process form data in HTML.

Form Validation

Form validation is the process of checking that user input is valid before it is submitted.

There are various techniques that you can use to validate user input in HTML, including client-side and server-side validation.

Client-side validation is performed by the web browser, and it is generally faster and more efficient than server-side validation. However, it is also less secure, as users can disable or bypass client-side validation.

Server-side validation is performed by the web server, and it is generally slower and less efficient than client-side validation. However, it is also more secure, as users cannot disable or bypass server-side validation.

HTML provides various attributes that you can use to validate user input, including:

- required: specifies that the input field is required
- pattern: specifies a regular expression that the input field must match
- min and max: specify the minimum and maximum values that the input field can have

Here's an example of how to use the required attribute to validate user input in HTML:

```
<input type="text" name="username"
placeholder="Enter your username" required>
```

In this example, we have added the required attribute to the input field, which specifies that the input field is required and that the user must enter a value.

Here's an example of how to use the pattern attribute to validate user input in HTML:

```
<input type="text" name="email"
placeholder="Enter your email"
pattern="[a-z0-9._%+-]+@[a-z0-9.-]+\.[a-z]{2,}$">
```

In this example, we have added the pattern attribute to the input field, which specifies a regular expression that the input field must match. In this case, the regular expression specifies that the input must be a valid email address.

Here's an example of how to use the min and max attributes to validate user input in HTML:

```
<input type="number" name="age"
placeholder="Enter your age" min="18" max="120">
```

In this example, we have added the min and max attributes to the input field, which specify the minimum and maximum values that the input field can have. In this case, the input field can only accept values between 18 and 120.

Form Processing

Form processing is the process of handling the user input after it has been submitted.

There are various techniques that you can use to process user input in HTML, including client-side and server-side processing.

Client-side processing is performed by the web browser, and it is generally faster and more efficient than server-side processing. However, it is also less secure, as users can disable or bypass client-side processing.

Server-side processing is performed by the web server, and it is generally slower and less efficient than client-side processing. However, it is also more secure, as users cannot disable or bypass server-side processing.

HTML provides various methods that you can use to process user input, including:

- GET: sends the data in the form as a query string in the URL
- POST: sends the data in the form as a request body

Here's an example of how to use the POST method to process user input in HTML:

```
<form action="/process-form.php" method="post">
  <input type="text" name="username" placeholder="Enter your username">
  <input type="password" name="password" placeholder="Enter your password">
  <button type="submit">Log in</button>
</form>
```

In this example, we have specified the POST method in the form using the method attribute, and we have specified the URL of the script that will process the form using the action attribute. When the user submits the form, the data will be sent as a request body to the specified URL.

On the server side, you can use a programming language like PHP or Python to process the form data. Here's an example of how to process form data using PHP:

```php
<?php
$username = $_POST['username'];
$password = $_POST['password'];
// Process the form data
// ...
?>
```

In this example, we have accessed the form data using the $_POSTsuperglobal array, which contains the form data as an associative array. We have then assigned the values of the username and password fields to variables for further processing.

Form Security

Form security is the process of protecting user input from unauthorized access and tampering.

There are various techniques that you can use to secure form data in HTML, including:

- Encrypting the data using SSL/TLS
- Validating the data using server-side validation
- Protecting against cross-site scripting (XSS) attacks using input sanitation

Here's an example of how to use SSL/TLS to secure form data in HTML:

```html
<form action="/process-form.php" method="post" enctype="multipart/form-data" accept-charset="UTF-8" onsubmit="return validateForm()">
    <input type="text" name="username" placeholder="Enter your username">
    <input type="password" name="password" placeholder="Enter your password">
    <button type="submit">Log in</button>
</form>
```

In this example, we have added the enctype and accept-charsetattributes to the form, which specify the encoding type and accepted character set for the form data. We have also added a JavaScript function to the onsubmit attribute to validate the form before it is submitted.

Conclusion

Validating and processing form data is an essential part of any web page that requires user input, and it allows you to ensure that user input is valid and properly handled before it is submitted. With the skills and knowledge you gain in this course, you'll be able to create professional-quality forms that are easy to use and secure.

Exercises

To review these concepts, we will go through a series of exercises designed to test your understanding and apply what you have learned.

What attribute is used to specify that an input field is required in HTML?

What attribute is used to specify a regular expression that an input field must match in HTML?
What attribute is used to specify the minimum and maximum
values that an input field can have in HTML?
What HTTP method is used to send the data in the form as a query string in the URL in HTML?
What HTTP method is used to send the data in the form as a request body in HTML?

Solutions

What attribute is used to specify that an input field is required in HTML?
The required attribute is used to specify that an input field is required in HTML.

What attribute is used to specify a regular expression that an input field must match in HTML?
The pattern attribute is used to specify a regular expression that an input field must match in HTML.

**What attribute is used to specify the minimum and maximum
values that an input field can have in HTML?**
The min and max attributes are used to specify the minimum and maximum values that an input field can have in HTML.

What HTTP method is used to send the data in the form as a query string in the URL in HTML?
The GET method is used to send the data in the form as a query string in the URL in HTML.

What HTTP method is used to send the data in the form as a request body in HTML?
The POST method is used to send the data in the form as a request body in HTML.

WORKING WITH FRAMES AND IFRAMES

Frames and iFrames are HTML elements that allow you to display multiple HTML documents within a single web page. They are useful for displaying content from external sources, such as other websites or local files.

In this article, we'll take a closer look at how to work with frames and iFrames in HTML.

Frames

Frames are HTML elements that allow you to divide a web page into multiple sections, each of which can display a different HTML document.

Here's an example of how to create a frame layout in HTML:

```
<frameset cols="25%,50%,25%">
  <frame src="frame1.html">
  <frame src="frame2.html">
  <frame src="frame3.html">
</frameset>
```

n this example, we have used the <frameset> element to define a frame layout with three columns, and we have used the <frame> element to specify the HTML documents that will be displayed in each column.

You can also specify the size of the frames using the rows and colsattributes of the <frameset> element. For example, you can use the colsattribute to specify the width of each frame as a percentage of the total width of the frame layout.

Here's an example of how to create a frame layout with fixed-size frames in HTML:

```
<frameset rows="100,200,300">
  <frame src="frame1.html">
  <frame src="frame2.html">
  <frame src="frame3.html">
</frameset>
```

In this example, we have used the rows attribute to specify the height of each frame in pixels.

You can also use the <noframes> element to provide an alternative content for users who do not have a frame-capable browser.

Here's an example of how to use the <noframes> element in HTML:

```
<frameset cols="25%,50%,25%">
 <frame src="frame1.html">
 <frame src="frame2.html">
 <frame src="frame3.html">
 <noframes>
  <p>Sorry, your browser does not support frames.</p>
 </noframes>
</frameset>
```

In this example, we have used the <noframes> element to provide an alternative content for users who do not have a frame-capable browser.

iFrames

iFrames are HTML elements that allow you to embed an HTML document within another HTML document. They are useful for displaying content from external sources, such as other websites or local files.

Here's an example of how to create an iFrame in HTML:

```
<iframe src="http://www.example.com"
width="500" height="300"></iframe>
```

In this example, we have used the <iframe> element to specify the source of the HTML document that will be displayed, as well as the width and height of the iFrame.

You can also use the frameborder attribute to specify whether the iFrame should have a border. For example, you can set the frameborder attribute to 0 to disable the border.

Here's an example of how to create an iFrame with no border in HTML:

```
<iframe src="http://www.example.com"
width="500" height="300" frameborder="0"></iframe>
```

In this example, we have set the frameborder attribute to 0 to disable the border for the iFrame.

You can also use the scrolling attribute to specify whether the iFrame should have scrollbars. For example, you can set the scrolling attribute to yes to enable scrollbars.

Here's an example of how to create an iFrame with scrollbars in HTML:

```
<iframe src="http://www.example.com" width="500" height="300" scrolling="yes"></iframe>
```

In this example, we have set the scrolling attribute to yes to enable scrollbars for the iFrame.

You can also use the name attribute to give the iFrame a unique name, which can be used to reference the iFrame from other parts of the HTML document.

Here's an example of how to create an iFrame with a unique name in HTML:

```
<iframe src="http://www.example.com" width="500" height="300" name="myiframe"></iframe>
```

In this example, we have given the iFrame the name myiframe using the name attribute.

Frame Security

Frame security is the process of protecting web pages and content from unauthorized access and tampering.

There are various techniques that you can use to secure frames and iFrames in HTML, including:

- Using the X-Frame-Options HTTP header to prevent clickjacking attacks
- Disabling JavaScript in the frames and iFrames
- Using the sandbox attribute to restrict the actions that can be performed in the frames and iFrames

Here's an example of how to use the X-Frame-Options HTTP header to prevent clickjacking attacks in HTML:

```
<meta http-equiv="X-Frame-Options" content="DENY">
```

In this example, we have used the X-Frame-Options HTTP header to specify that the page should not be displayed in a frame.

Here's an example of how to disable JavaScript in frames and iFrames in HTML:

In this example, we have used the sandbox attribute to disable JavaScript in the iFrame.

Conclusion

Frames and iFrames are powerful HTML elements that allow you to display multiple HTML documents within a single web page. With the skills and knowledge you gain in this course, you'll be able to create professional-quality web pages that use frames and iFrames effectively.

Exercises

To review these concepts, we will go through a series of exercises designed to test your understanding and apply what you have learned.

What element is used to define a frame layout in HTML?
What element is used to specify the HTML documents that will
be displayed in a frame layout in HTML?
What element is used to embed an HTML document within another HTML document in HTML?
What attribute is used to specify whether the iFrame should have scrollbars in HTML?

What attribute is used to give an iFrame a unique name in HTML?

Solutions

What element is used to define a frame layout in HTML?

The <frameset> element is used to define a frame layout in HTML.

What element is used to specify the HTML documents that will be displayed in a frame layout in HTML?

The <frame> element is used to specify the HTML documents that will be displayed in a frame layout in HTML.

What element is used to embed an HTML document within another HTML document in HTML?

The <iframe> element is used to embed an HTML document within another HTML document in HTML.

What attribute is used to specify whether the iFrame should have scrollbars in HTML?

The scrolling attribute is used to specify whether the iFrame should have scrollbars in HTML.

What attribute is used to give an iFrame a unique name in HTML?

The name attribute is used to give an iFrame a unique name in HTML. For example:

```
<iframe src="http://www.example.com" width="500"
height="300" name="myiframe"></iframe>
```

In this example, we have given the iFrame the name myiframe using the name attribute.

USING HTML5 SEMANTIC TAGS

HTML5 introduced a number of new semantic tags that allow you to add meaning and structure to your HTML documents. These tags help to improve the accessibility and readability of your web pages, and they make it easier for search engines to understand the content of your pages.

In this article, we'll take a closer look at how to use HTML5 semantic tags in your web pages.

HTML5 Semantic Tags

HTML5 semantic tags are HTML elements that are used to define the different parts of an HTML document, such as the header, footer, main content, and navigation.

Here's a list of some of the most commonly used HTML5 semantic tags:

- <header>: Defines the header of a web page
- <footer>: Defines the footer of a web page
- <main>: Defines the main content of a web page
- <nav>: Defines a section of the web page that contains navigation links
- <article>: Defines an independent piece of content, such as a blog post or news article
- <section>: Defines a section of the web page that contains related content
- <aside>: Defines content that is related to the main content of the web page, but is separate from it
- <figure>: Defines a group of content, such as an image or video, that is self-contained and can be moved around the page

Here's an example of how to use HTML5 semantic tags in an HTML document:

```
<header>
<h1>My Website</h1>
<nav>
 <ul>
  <li><a href="#">Home</a></li>
  <li><a href="#">About</a></li>
  <li><a href="#">Contact</a></li>
 </ul>
</nav>
</header>
<main>
```

```
<article>
  <h2>Welcome to My Website</h2>
  <p>Lorem ipsum dolor sit amet, consectetur adipiscing elit. Integer aliquam nunc vel est iaculis, eu
ornare lacus tincidunt.</p>
</article>
<aside>
  <h3>Related Links</h3>
  <ul>
    <li><a href="#">Link 1</a></li>
    <li><a href="#">Link 2</a></li>
    <li><a href="#">Link 3</a></li>
  </ul>
</aside>
</main>
<footer>
  <p>Copyright 2021 My Website</p>
</footer>
```

In this example, we have used the <header>, <main>, <article>, <aside>, and <footer> tags to structure the HTML document. The <header>element contains the website's logo and navigation links, the <main>element contains the main content of the web page, the <article>element contains a standalone piece of content, the <aside> element contains related content, and the <footer> element contains the website's copyright information.

HTML5 Semantic Tags and SEO

Using HTML5 semantic tags can improve the SEO (Search Engine Optimization) of your web pages. SEO is the process of optimizing your web pages to rank higher in search engine results pages (SERPs).

Search engines use algorithms to crawl and index web pages, and they use various factors to determine the relevance and quality of a web page. One of these factors is the use of HTML5 semantic tags, which help search engines understand the structure and content of a web page.

By using HTML5 semantic tags, you can help search engines understand the purpose and content of different parts of your web pages. This can improve the ranking of your web pages in search engine results pages, and it can also increase the chances of your web pages being shown as rich snippets in search results.

Conclusion

HTML5 semantic tags are a powerful tool for adding meaning and structure to your HTML documents. By using these tags, you can improve the accessibility, readability, and SEO of your web pages.

Exercises

To review these concepts, we will go through a series of exercises designed to test your understanding and apply what you have learned.

Which HTML5 semantic tag is used to define the main content of a web page?
Which HTML5 semantic tag is used to define an independent piece
of content, such as a blog post or news article?
Which HTML5 semantic tag is used to define a group of content, such as an image
or video, that is self-contained and can be moved around the page?
Can HTML5 semantic tags improve the SEO of a web page?
Which HTML5 semantic tag is used to define a section of the
web page that contains related content?

Solutions

Which HTML5 semantic tag is used to define the main content of a web page?
The <main> tag is used to define the main content of a web page.

Which HTML5 semantic tag is used to define an independent piece
of content, such as a blog post or news article?
The <article> tag is used to define an independent piece of content, such as a blog post or news article.

Which HTML5 semantic tag is used to define a group of content, such as an image
or video, that is self-contained and can be moved around the page?
The <figure> tag is used to define a group of content, such as an image or video, that is self-contained and can be moved around the page.

Can HTML5 semantic tags improve the SEO of a web page?
Yes, HTML5 semantic tags can improve the SEO of a web page by helping search engines understand the structure and content of the page. This can improve the ranking of the web page in search engine results pages and increase the chances of the web page being shown as a rich snippet in search results.

Which HTML5 semantic tag is used to define a section of the
web page that contains related content?
The <section> tag is used to define a section of the web page that contains related content. For example:

```html
<section>
<h2>Section Title</h2>
<p>Lorem ipsum onec ullamcorper tempus mauris, a convallis dolor viverra quis.</p>
</section>
```

In this example, we have used the <section> tag to define a section of the web page that contains a title and a paragraph of related content.

CREATING MULTIMEDIA CONTENT WITH AUDIO AND VIDEO ELEMENTS

The HTML <audio> and <video> elements allow you to add multimedia content, such as audio and video files, to your web pages. These elements make it easy to play audio and video files directly in the browser, without the need for external plugins or applications.

In this article, we'll take a closer look at how to use the <audio> and <video> elements in your HTML documents.

The <audio> Element

The <audio> element is used to embed an audio file in an HTML document. Here's an example of how to use the <audio> element:

```
<audio src="audio.mp3" controls></audio>
```

In this example, we have used the src attribute to specify the location of the audio file, and the controls attribute to add controls to the audio player. The controls attribute allows the user to play, pause, and adjust the volume of the audio.

You can also use the <audio> element to specify multiple audio sources, in case the browser doesn't support a particular audio format. For example:

```
<audio controls>
  <source src="audio.mp3" type="audio/mpeg">
  <source src="audio.ogg" type="audio/ogg">
  Your browser does not support the audio element.
</audio>
```

n this example, we have provided both an MP3 and an OGG audio file as sources. If the browser doesn't support MP3 files, it will try to play the OGG file instead. The text inside the <audio> element is displayed if the browser doesn't support the <audio> element at all.

The <video> Element

The <video> element is used to embed a video file in an HTML document. Here's an example of how to use the <video> element:

```
<video src="video.mp4" width="640"
height="360" controls></video>
```

In this example, we have used the src attribute to specify the location of the video file, and the width and height attributes to specify the size of the video player. We have also used the controls attribute to add controls to the video player.

Like the <audio> element, you can use the <video> element to specify multiple video sources, in case the browser doesn't support a particular video format. For example:

```
<video width="640" height="360" controls>
<source src="video.mp4" type="video/mp4">
<source src="video.webm" type="video/webm">
Your browser does not support the video element.
</video>
```

In this example, we have provided both an MP4 and a WEBM video file as sources. If the browser doesn't support MP4 files, it will try to play the WEBM file instead. The text inside the <video> element is displayed if the browser doesn't support the <video> element at all.

The <source> Element

The <source> element is used inside the <audio> and <video> elements to specify multiple sources for the audio or video file. The <source>element has two attributes: src and type. The src attribute specifies the location of the audio or video file, and the type attribute specifies the MIME type of the file.

Here's an example of how to use the <source> element:

```
<video width="640" height="360" controls>
<source src="video.mp4" type="video/mp4">
<source src="video.webm" type="video/webm">
Your browser does not support the video element.
</video>
```

In this example, we have used the <source> element to specify two video sources: an MP4 file and a WEBM file. The browser will try to play the first source that it supports. If it doesn't support any of the sources, it will display the text inside the <video> element.

The <track> Element

The <track> element is used inside the <audio> and <video> elements to specify a text track for the audio or video file. The <track> element has several attributes:

- src: The location of the text track file
- kind: The kind of text track (e.g. subtitles, captions, descriptions)

- srclang: The language of the text track
- label: The label for the text track

Here's an example of how to use the <track> element:

```
<video width="640" height="360" controls>
  <source src="video.mp4" type="video/mp4">
  <source src="video.webm" type="video/webm">
  <track src="captions.vtt" kind="captions" srclang="en" label="English">
  Your browser does not support the video element.
</video>
```

In this example, we have used the <track> element to specify an English caption track for the video file. The caption track is a separate file in the WebVTT format. The kind attribute specifies that the track is a caption track, the srclang attribute specifies the language of the track, and the label attribute provides a label for the track.

Conclusion

The <audio> and <video> elements, along with the <source> and <track>elements, make it easy

to add multimedia content to your web pages. These elements allow you to play audio and video files directly in the browser, without the need for external plugins or applications.

Remember to always use the appropriate audio and video formats that are supported by the majority of browsers. You can use the <source> element to specify multiple sources in different formats, so that the browser can choose the one that it supports.

Additionally, you can use the <track> element to provide text tracks for audio and video files, such as subtitles or captions. This can improve the accessibility of your multimedia content for users with hearing impairments or for those who prefer to watch a video with captions.

I hope this article has helped you learn how to use the <audio>, <video>, <source>, and <track> elements in your HTML documents. With these elements, you can easily add multimedia content to your web pages and improve the user experience for your visitors.

Exercises

To review these concepts, we will go through a series of exercises designed to test your understanding and apply what you have learned.

Which HTML element is used to embed an audio file in an HTML document?
Which HTML element is used to specify multiple sources for an audio or video file?
How do you add controls to an <audio> **element?**
What is the <track> **element used for?**
What is the srclang **attribute used for in the** <track>**element?**

Solutions

Which HTML element is used to embed an audio file in an HTML document?

The <audio> element is used to embed an audio file in an HTML document.

Which HTML element is used to specify multiple sources for an audio or video file?

The <source> element is used to specify multiple sources for an audio or video file.

How do you add controls to an <audio> **element?**

You can add controls to an <audio> element by using the controlsattribute. For example: <audio src="audio.mp3" controls></audio>

What is the <track> **element used for?**

The <track> element is used to specify a text track for an audio or video file. It can be used to provide subtitles, captions, or descriptions for the audio or video.

What is the srclang **attribute used for in the** <track>**element?**

The srclang attribute in the <track> element is used to specify the language of the text track. For example: <track src="captions.vtt" kind="captions" srclang="en" label="English">

USING HTML APIS AND WEB COMPONENTS

HTML APIs and web components are powerful tools that allow you to extend the functionality of your HTML documents and create reusable components for your web applications.

In this article, we'll take a closer look at what HTML APIs and web components are, how they work, and how you can use them in your web development projects.

What are HTML APIs?

HTML APIs, or Application Programming Interfaces, are a set of programming instructions that allow you to interact with external resources or services from within your HTML documents.

There are many different HTML APIs available, each with its own specific functionality. Some common examples include:

- The Geolocation API, which allows you to access the user's location information
- The Canvas API, which allows you to draw graphics and animations on a web page
- The Web Storage API, which allows you to store data in the browser's local storage

To use an HTML API, you simply need to include the appropriate script in your HTML document and call the API's functions as needed.

For example, to use the Geolocation API to get the user's current location, you can use the following code:

```
<script>
function getLocation() {
 if (navigator.geolocation) {
   navigator.geolocation.getCurrentPosition(showPosition);
 } else {
   alert("Geolocation is not supported by this browser.");
 }
}
function showPosition(position) {
 alert("Latitude: " + position.coords.latitude +
   "Longitude: " + position.coords.longitude);
```

```
}
```

```
</script>
```

```
<button onclick="getLocation()">Get my location</button>
```

In this example, we have used the getCurrentPosition function of the Geolocation API to get the user's current location and display it in an alert.

What are Web Components?

Web components are a set of standardized APIs that allow you to create reusable components for your web applications.

Web components consist of three main technologies:

- Custom Elements: Allow you to define your own HTML elements with custom functionality
- Shadow DOM: Allows you to encapsulate the styles and DOM structure of a component, so that it doesn't conflict with the rest of the page
- HTML Templates: Allows you to define reusable templates for your components

With web components, you can create custom elements with their own functionality and styles, and use them as if they were regular HTML elements.

For example, let's say you want to create a custom button element that displays a loading spinner when clicked. You can define the button element using the Custom Elements API like this:

```
<template id="loading-button-template">
  <style>
    /* Add styles for the loading button */
  </style>
  <button>
    <slot></slot>
  </button>
</template>
<script>
class LoadingButton extends HTMLElement {
  constructor() {
    super();
    // Create a shadow root
    this.attachShadow({ mode: 'open' });
    // Clone the template and add it to the shadow root
    const template = document.querySelector('#loading-button-template');
    const instance = template.content.cloneNode(true);
```

```
this.shadowRoot.appendChild(instance);
// Get a reference to the button element
this.button = this.shadowRoot.querySelector('button');
// Add an event listener for the click event
this.button.addEventListener('click', () => {
  // Show the loading spinner and disable the button
  this.button.innerHTML = 'Loading...';
  this.button.disabled = true;
});
}
}
// Define the custom element
customElements.define('loading-button', LoadingButton);
</script>
```

Now you can use the <loading-button> element in your HTML documents like this:

When clicked, the button will display a loading spinner and disable itself until the action is complete.

Conclusion

HTML APIs and web components are powerful tools that allow you to extend the functionality of your HTML documents and create reusable components for your web applications. By using these technologies, you can create more interactive and user-friendly web pages, and improve the overall user experience for your visitors.

Exercises

To review these concepts, we will go through a series of exercises designed to test your understanding and apply what you have learned.

What are HTML APIs used for?
What are the three main technologies that make up web components?
How do you create a custom element using the Custom Elements API?
How do you create a shadow root for a custom element?
How do you define a reusable template for a custom element using the HTML Templates API?

Solutions

What are HTML APIs used for?
HTML APIs, or Application Programming Interfaces, are a set of programming instructions that allow you to interact with external resources or services from within your HTML documents.

What are the three main technologies that make up web components?
The three main technologies that make up web components are Custom Elements, Shadow DOM,

and HTML Templates.

How do you create a custom element using the Custom Elements API?

To create a custom element using the Custom Elements API, you need to define a class that extends the HTMLElement class and define the custom element using the customElements.define function. For example:

```
class MyCustomElement extends HTMLElement {
  // Custom element functionality goes here
}
customElements.define('my-custom-element', MyCustomElement);
```

How do you create a shadow root for a custom element?

To create a shadow root for a custom element, you can use the attachShadow function and pass it an options object with the mode set to 'open'. For example:

```
this.attachShadow({ mode: 'open' });
```

How do you define a reusable template for a custom element using the HTML Templates API?

To define a reusable template for a custom element using the HTML Templates API, you can use the <template> element and give it an idattribute. You can then clone the template and add it to the shadow root of your custom element using the content.cloneNode function. For example:

```
<template id="my-template">
  <!-- Template content goes here -->
</template>
<script>
  const template = document.querySelector('#my-template');
  const instance = template.content.cloneNode(true);
  this.shadowRoot.appendChild(instance);
</script>
```

TIPS FOR WRITING CLEAN, MAINTAINABLE HTML CODE

Writing clean and maintainable HTML code is crucial for building efficient and scalable web applications. By following best practices and adopting good coding habits, you can make your HTML code more organized, easy to read, and easier to maintain.

In this article, we'll explore some tips and techniques for writing clean and maintainable HTML code.

Use Semantic HTML Elements

One of the most important aspects of writing clean HTML code is using semantic HTML elements. Semantic HTML elements are tags that describe the meaning and purpose of their content, rather than just defining its appearance.

For example, instead of using a <div> element to define a section of content, you should use a more specific semantic element such as <header>, <footer>, <article>, or <section>. This helps to improve the accessibility of your web page, as well as making the HTML easier to understand and maintain.

Here's an example of using semantic elements to structure a basic page layout:

```
<header>
 <h1>Page Title</h1>
</header>
<nav>
 <ul>
  <li><a href="#">Home</a></li>
  <li><a href="#">About</a></li>
  <li><a href="#">Contact</a></li>
 </ul>
</nav>
<main>
 <article>
  <h2>Article Title</h2>
  <p>Article content goes here</p>
 </article>
```

```
</main>
<footer>
  <p>Copyright 2021</p>
</footer>
```

In this example, we have used semantic elements to define the header, navigation, main content, and footer sections of the page. This makes the HTML more meaningful and easier to understand, and helps to improve the accessibility of the page.

Use Descriptive and Meaningful Class and ID Names

Another important aspect of writing clean HTML code is using descriptive and meaningful class and ID names. Class and ID names should clearly describe the purpose of the element they are applied to, and should be easy to read and understand.

For example, instead of using a class name like .red, you should use a more descriptive name such as .error-message or .highlighted. This helps to improve the readability and maintainability of your HTML code, as well as making it easier to understand the purpose of each element.

Here's an example of using descriptive class names to style a form:

```
<form>
  <label for="name" class="form-label">Name:</label>
  <input type="text" id="name" class="form-input">
  <label for="email" class="form-label">Email:</label>
  <input type="email" id="email" class="form-input">
  <label for="message" class="form-label">Message:</label>
  <textarea id="message" class="form-textarea"></textarea>
  <button type="submit" class="form-button">Send</button>
</form>
```

In this example, we have used descriptive class names such as form-label, form-input, form-textarea, and form-button to style the form elements. This makes the HTML more meaningful and easier to understand, and allows us to easily identify the purpose of each class.

Use Proper Indentation and Spacing

Proper indentation and spacing is another important aspect of writing clean HTML code. By using consistent indentation and spacing, you can make your HTML code more organized and easier to read.

For example, you should indent nested elements to clearly indicate their hierarchy and use multiple lines to separate different sections of code. This helps to improve the readability and maintainability of your HTML code, and makes it easier to spot errors and debug issues.

Here's an example of using proper indentation and spacing to structure a list of items:

```
<ul>
<li>Item 1</li>
<li>Item 2</li>
<li>
  Item 3
  <ul>
    <li>Subitem 1</li>
    <li>Subitem 2</li>
  </ul>
</li>
</ul>
```

In this example, we have used indentation to clearly indicate the hierarchy of the list items and their subitems. This makes the HTML more organized and easier to read, and helps to improve the overall maintainability of the code.

Use Lowercase and Minified HTML

To improve the performance and maintainability of your HTML code, you should use lowercase tags and attributes, and minify your HTML whenever possible.

Lowercasing your HTML tags and attributes makes your code more consistent and easier to read, and minifying your HTML removes unnecessary whitespace and comments, reducing the file size and improving the loading speed of your web pages.

Here's an example of minified HTML:

```
<!DOCTYPE html><html lang="en"><head><title>Page Title</title></head><body><h1>Hello World</h1></body></html>
```

Conclusion

By following these tips and techniques, you can write clean and maintainable HTML code that is organized, easy to read, and easier to maintain. By using semantic HTML elements, descriptive and meaningful class and ID names, proper indentation and spacing, and lowercase and minified HTML, you can improve the quality and efficiency of your HTML code and create better web applications for your users.

Exercises

To review these concepts, we will go through a series of exercises designed to test your understanding and apply what you have learned.

Write the HTML code for a simple page layout that includes a header, navigation, main content, and footer. Use semantic HTML elements to structure the page.

Write the HTML code for a simple form that includes a name input, email input, message

textarea, and submit button. Use descriptive class names to style the form elements.
Write the HTML code for a simple list of items that includes multiple levels of
nested items. Use proper indentation and spacing to structure the list.
Write the HTML code for a simple page layout that includes a header, navigation, main
content, and footer. Use the div element and appropriate class names to structure the page.
Write the HTML code for a simple form that includes a name input, email input, message textarea,
and submit button. Use the div element and appropriate class names to structure the form.

Solutions

Write the HTML code for a simple page layout that includes a header, navigation,
main content, and footer. Use semantic HTML elements to structure the page.

```html
<html>
<head>
 <title>My Page</title>
</head>
<body>
 <header>
  <h1>Page Title</h1>
 </header>
 <nav>
  <ul>
   <li><a href="#">Home</a></li>
   <li><a href="#">About</a></li>
   <li><a href="#">Contact</a></li>
  </ul>
 </nav>
 <main>
  <h2>Main Content</h2>
  <p>Welcome to my page!</p>
 </main>
 <footer>
  <p>Copyright 2021</p>
 </footer>
</body>
</html>
```

Write the HTML code for a simple form that includes a name input, email input, message
textarea, and submit button. Use descriptive class names to style the form elements.

```html
<form>
```

```
<label for="name" class="form-label">Name:</label>
<input type="text" id="name" class="form-input">
<label for="email" class="form-label">Email:</label>
<input type="email" id="email" class="form-input">
<label for="message" class="form-label">Message:</label>
<textarea id="message" class="form-textarea"></textarea>
<button type="submit" class="form-button">Send</button>
</form>
```

Write the HTML code for a simple list of items that includes multiple levels of nested items. Use proper indentation and spacing to structure the list.

```
<ul>
<li>Item 1</li>
<li>Item 2</li>
<li>
  Item 3
  <ul>
    <li>Subitem 1</li>
    <li>Subitem 2</li>
  </ul>
</li>
</ul>
```

Write the HTML code for a simple page layout that includes a header, navigation, main content, and footer. Use the div element and appropriate class names to structure the page.

```
<div class="page">
<div class="header">
  <h1>Page Title</h1>
</div>
<div class="navigation">
  <ul>
    <li><a href="#">Home</a></li>
    <li><a href="#">About</a></li>
    <li><a href="#">Contact</a></li>
  </ul>
</div>
<div class="main-content">
```

```
<h2>Main Content</h2>
```

```
<p>Welcome to my page!</p>
```

```
</div>
```

```
<div class="footer">
```

```
<p>Copyright 2021</p>
```

```
</div>
```

```
</div>
```

Write the HTML code for a simple form that includes a name input, email input, message textarea, and submit button. Use the div element and appropriate class names to structure the form.

```
<form>
```

```
<div class="form-group">
```

```
<label for="name" class="form-label">Name:</label>
```

```
<input type="text" id="name" class="form-input">
```

```
</div>
```

```
<div class="form-group">
```

```
<label for="email" class="form-label">Email:</label>
```

```
<input type="email" id="email" class="form-input">
```

```
</div>
```

```
<div class="form-group">
```

```
<label for="message" class="form-label">Message:</label>
```

```
<textarea id="message" class="form-textarea"></textarea>
```

```
</div>
```

```
<div class="form-group">
```

```
<button type="submit" class="form-button">Send</button>
```

```
</div>
```

```
</form>
```

COMMON HTML MISTAKES AND HOW TO AVOID THEM

As you start learning HTML and building websites, it's inevitable that you'll make mistakes. Whether it's a typo in your code, a missing closing tag, or a misunderstanding of how a particular element works, these mistakes can be frustrating and time-consuming to fix. In this article, we'll explore some common HTML mistakes and how you can avoid them as you learn and grow as a developer.

Not Closing Tags

One of the most basic mistakes you can make when writing HTML is forgetting to close a tag. Every opening tag must have a corresponding closing tag, with the exception of self-closing tags like <img> and <input>. If you forget to close a tag, it can cause all sorts of issues with your layout and formatting. To avoid this mistake, make sure you're in the habit of always closing your tags, and use a text editor or code editor that helps you keep track of your tags.

Misusing HTML Elements

Another common mistake is using the wrong HTML element for the job. For example, using a <p> element for a heading or using a <div> element for a list. It's important to familiarize yourself with the different HTML elements and their purpose so that you can use them correctly in your code. A good way to avoid this mistake is to consult the HTML documentation and practice using the different elements as you learn.

Not Nesting Elements Properly

Another common mistake is not nesting elements properly. In HTML, it's important to nest elements correctly to ensure that your code is valid and your layout is displayed correctly. For example, a list item should always be nested within a list element, and a heading should always be nested within a section element. To avoid this mistake, pay attention to the nesting of your elements and make sure they're nested correctly.

Not Using Descriptive Class and ID Names:

As you start using class and ID attributes to style your elements, it's important to use descriptive names that clearly indicate the purpose of the element. Using generic names like "class1" or "id1" can make it difficult to understand the purpose of the element, especially as your codebase grows. To avoid this mistake, take the time to come up with descriptive class and ID names that clearly indicate the purpose of the element.

Not Validating Your HTML:

As you write HTML, it's important to validate your code to ensure that it's free of errors and meets the standards of the language. There are a number of tools available that can help you validate your HTML, including the W3C Markup Validation Service. By taking the time to validate your HTML, you can catch mistakes early on and avoid problems down the road.

Conclusion

Making mistakes is a natural part of learning any new skill, and HTML is no exception. By being aware of some of the common mistakes that beginners make, you can avoid making them yourself and save yourself a lot of time and frustration. As you continue to learn and grow as a developer, keep these tips in mind and always be willing to ask for help when you need it.

Exercises

To review these concepts, we will go through a series of exercises designed to test your understanding and apply what you have learned.

Explain what happens when you forget to close a tag in HTML.
List three common mistakes you can make when using HTML elements.
Describe a scenario where using a <div> **element instead of**
a <table> **element might cause problems with your layout.**
Explain what it means to nest elements properly in HTML.
Describe a scenario where using descriptive class and ID names can be helpful.

Solutions

Explain what happens when you forget to close a tag in HTML.

When you forget to close a tag in HTML, it can cause all sorts of issues with your layout and formatting. The browser may not be able to properly interpret the rest of the HTML code and may display the content incorrectly or not at all. This can be frustrating and time-consuming to fix, as you may need to go back and search through your code to find the unclosed tag. To avoid this mistake, make sure you're in the habit of always closing your tags and use a text editor or code editor that helps you keep track of your tags.

List three common mistakes you can make when using HTML elements.

1. Using the wrong HTML element for the job.
2. Not nesting elements properly.
3. Using generic class and ID names.

Describe a scenario where using a <div> **element instead of**
a <table> **element might cause problems with your layout.**

If you are trying to create a tabular layout with rows and columns, using a <div> element instead of a <table> element might cause problems with your layout. The <div> element is not designed for this purpose, and you may have difficulty getting the elements to align properly in the desired rows and columns. Instead, you should use the <table> element, which is specifically designed for creating tabular layouts.

Explain what it means to nest elements properly in HTML.

In HTML, it's important to nest elements properly to ensure that your code is valid and your layout is displayed correctly. This means that each element should be properly contained within the appropriate parent element. For example, a list item should always be nested within a list element, and a heading should always be nested within a section element. Failing to nest elements properly can lead to problems with your layout and may cause your code to be invalid.

Describe a scenario where using descriptive class and ID names can be helpful.

Using descriptive class and ID names can be helpful when you are working on a large codebase with many different elements. By using names that clearly indicate the purpose of the element, it's easier to understand the function and purpose of each element, especially when working with other developers. This can make it easier to maintain and update your code, as well as troubleshoot any issues that may arise. On the other hand, using generic names like "class1" or "id1" can make it difficult to understand the purpose of the element, especially as your codebase grows.

DEBUGGING AND TESTING
HTML CODE

As you start building websites with HTML, it's important to have a process in place for debugging and testing your code. Even the most experienced developers make mistakes from time to time, and it's important to have a plan in place for finding and fixing those mistakes. In this article, we'll explore some tools and techniques for debugging and testing HTML code, as well as some common issues you might encounter as you learn and grow as a developer.

Using a Code Editor or IDE

One of the first steps in debugging and testing your HTML code is to use a code editor or integrated development environment (IDE). These tools provide a variety of features that can help you write and debug your code, including syntax highlighting, code completion, and error checking. Some popular code editors and IDEs for HTML development include Atom, Sublime Text, and Visual Studio Code.

Validating Your HTML

Another important step in debugging and testing your HTML code is to validate it. This means checking your code against the standards of the language to ensure that it's free of errors and follows best practices. There are a number of tools available for validating HTML, including the W3C Markup Validation Service. By validating your HTML, you can catch mistakes early on and avoid problems down the road.

Using a Browser DevTools

Another useful tool for debugging and testing HTML code is a browser's devtools. These tools allow you to inspect and debug your code in real-time, and can be a valuable resource for finding and fixing errors. To access devtools in most browsers, you can use the F12 key or right-click on an element and select "Inspect".

Debugging Common HTML Issues

As you start building websites with HTML, you'll likely encounter a number of common issues. Here are a few examples:

- Missing closing tags: As mentioned earlier, it's important to make sure that you close all of your tags in HTML. If you forget to close a tag, it can cause problems with your layout and formatting.
- Misusing HTML elements: Another common mistake is using the wrong HTML element

for the job. For example, using a <p> element for a heading or using a <div> element for a list. It's important to familiarize yourself with the different HTML elements and their purpose so that you can use them correctly in your code.

- Not nesting elements properly: In HTML, it's important to nest elements correctly to ensure that your code is valid and your layout is displayed correctly. For example, a list item should always be nested within a list element, and a heading should always be nested within a section element.

Testing Your HTML Code

Once you've debugged your HTML code and fixed any errors, it's important to test it to ensure that it's functioning as intended. There are a number of ways to test your HTML code, including:

- Using a browser to view your code: One of the simplest ways to test your HTML code is to load it into a browser and see how it looks. This can give you an idea of how your code will be interpreted by different browsers and devices.
- Using a testing framework: Another option is to use a testing framework like Selenium or PhantomJS. These tools allow you to automate testing and ensure that your code is functioning correctly across different browsers and devices.
- Using a testing service: Finally, you can use a testing service like BrowserStack or Sauce Labs to test your code on a variety of different browsers and devices. These services provide a range of tools and features for testing and debugging your code, and can be a valuable resource for ensuring that your website is fully functional and accessible to all users.

Conclusion

Debugging and testing HTML code is an important part of the website development process. By using tools like code editors, browser devtools, and testing frameworks, you can ensure that your code is free of errors and functions as intended. Additionally, it's important to familiarize yourself with common HTML mistakes and best practices to avoid these issues as you continue to learn and grow as a developer. With the right tools and techniques, you'll be able to build professional, high-quality websites that are functional, accessible, and easy to maintain.

Exercises

To review these concepts, we will go through a series of exercises designed to test your understanding and apply what you have learned.

What is the purpose of validating HTML code?
List three tools or techniques that can be used for debugging HTML code.
What is the purpose of using a testing framework like Selenium or PhantomJS?
What is the difference between a code editor and an IDE?
What are some common issues you might encounter when working with HTML code?

Solutions

What is the purpose of validating HTML code?
The purpose of validating HTML code is to check it against the standards of the language to ensure that it is free of errors and follows best practices. By validating your HTML, you can catch mistakes

early on and avoid problems down the road.

List three tools or techniques that can be used for debugging HTML code.
1. A code editor or IDE
2. A browser's devtools
3. A testing framework

What is the purpose of using a testing framework like Selenium or PhantomJS?

The purpose of using a testing framework like Selenium or PhantomJS is to automate testing and ensure that your HTML code is functioning correctly across different browsers and devices. These tools allow you to create automated test cases and run them on various browsers and devices, helping you to ensure that your website is fully functional and accessible to all users.

What is the difference between a code editor and an IDE?

A code editor is a tool that is specifically designed for writing and editing code. It typically provides features like syntax highlighting, code completion, and error checking to help you write and debug your code. An integrated development environment (IDE) is a more comprehensive tool that includes features like a code editor, as well as additional tools and features for building and debugging code. An IDE may include features like a debugger, version control integration, and support for multiple programming languages.

What are some common issues you might encounter when working with HTML code?

Some common issues you might encounter when working with HTML code include:

- Missing closing tags
- Misusing HTML elements
- Not nesting elements properly
- Incorrectly formatted attributes
- Syntax errors
- Compatibility issues with different browsers and devices

BUILDING A COMPLETE
HTML WEBSITE

Now that you've learned the basics of HTML, it's time to put your skills to the test and build a complete website from scratch. In this article, we'll walk through the process of building a simple HTML website, covering everything from planning and layout to coding and testing. By the end of this tutorial, you'll have a fully functional website that you can use as a template for future projects.

Planning Your Website

The first step in building a website is to plan out what you want it to include. This might include the layout, content, and any special features or functionality that you want to include. Some things to consider when planning your website include:

- The purpose of your website: What do you want your website to achieve? Is it a personal blog, a business website, or something else entirely?
- Your target audience: Who do you want to visit your website? What are their interests and needs, and how can you cater to them with your content and design?
- The content of your website: What information do you want to include on your website? Do you have text, images, videos, or other media that you want to feature?
- The layout of your website: How do you want your website to look? Do you want a simple, single-page layout, or do you want to include multiple pages with navigation links?

Designing Your Website

Once you have a clear idea of what you want your website to include, it's time to start designing it. This might involve creating a wireframe or mockup of your website to get a sense of the layout and design. Some things to consider when designing your website include:

- The color scheme: What colors do you want to use on your website? Consider how the colors will work together and what mood or feeling you want to convey.
- The font: What font do you want to use for your website? Consider the readability and style of the font, as well as how it will work with your color scheme.
- The layout: How do you want your website to be structured? Will you have a header, footer, and sidebars, or will you use a more minimal layout?
- The navigation: How will users navigate around your website? Will you include a menu with links to different pages, or will you use a single-page layout with anchors to jump between sections?

Coding Your Website

Once you have a clear plan and design for your website, it's time to start coding it. This will involve writing the HTML, CSS, and any other code that you need to build your website. Some things to keep in mind as you code your website include:

- Using proper HTML syntax: Make sure to use the correct tags and attributes for your HTML elements, and close all of your tags properly.
- Structuring your HTML correctly: Use the correct hierarchy of HTML elements to ensure that your website is semantically correct and easy to understand.
- Using CSS to style your website: Use CSS to apply colors, fonts, and other styles to your website to make it look the way you want.

Testing Your Website

Once you've coded your website, it's important to test it to ensure that it's functioning as intended. This might involve checking for errors, testing the layout and design on different browsers and devices, and checking for usability issues. Some things to consider when testing your website include:

- Validating your HTML: Use a tool like the W3C Markup Validation Service to ensure that your HTML is free of errors and follows the standards of the language.
- Testing the layout and design: Use different browsers and devices to ensure that your website looks and functions as intended. This might include checking for responsive design issues and testing on different screen sizes.
- Checking for usability issues: Test your website to ensure that it's easy to use and navigate. Consider asking friends or colleagues to test it as well to get additional feedback.

Conclusion

Building a complete HTML website from scratch can seem like a daunting task, but with the right planning, design, and coding skills, it's a rewarding and achievable goal. By following the steps outlined in this tutorial, you'll be able to build a professional, functional website that meets your needs and goals. With practice and continued learning, you'll be able to build even more complex and sophisticated websites as you continue to grow as a developer.

Sample Project

Here is a skeleton of an HTML website if you need some help.

Sample HTML Website

```
<!DOCTYPE html>
<html>
<head>
    <title>My Website</title>
    <style>
        body {
            font-family: sans-serif;
```

```css
        color: #333;
    }
    header {
        background-color: #eee;
        padding: 20px;
    }
    nav {
        display: flex;
        justify-content: space-between;
    }
    nav a {
        color: #333;
        text-decoration: none;
        padding: 10px;
    }
    nav a:hover {
        color: #f60;
    }
    main {
        max-width: 800px;
        margin: 0 auto;
        padding: 20px;
    }
    h1, h2, h3 {
        color: #f60;
    }
    img {
        max-width: 100%;
    }
    footer {
        background-color: #eee;
        padding: 20px;
        text-align: center;
    }
    </style>
</head>
```

```
<body>
    <header>
        <h1>My Website</h1>
    </header>
    <nav>
        <a href="#">Home</a>
        <a href="#">About</a>
        <a href="#">Contact</a>
    </nav>
    <main>
        <h2>Welcome to My Website</h2>
        <p>Lorem ipsum dolor sit amet, consectetur adipiscing elit. Pellentesque eleifend lorem a metus ultricies, eu ullamcorper diam lobortis. Nunc at mauris volutpat, porta quam a, ultricies purus. Vivamus consectetur ligula sed neque fermentum, eu ultricies arcu convallis. Cras tincidunt magna id finibus cursus. Vestibulum at fringilla tellus, at facilisis dolor. Fusce mollis nisl non dui gravida, id congue est elementum. Nunc in metus varius, posuere felis et, hendrerit nisi.</p>
        <img src="https://via.placeholder.com/800x600" alt="Placeholder image">
        <h3>About Me</h3>
        <p>Lorem ipsum dolor sit amet, consectetur adipiscing elit. Pellentesque eleifend lorem a metus ultricies, eu ullamcorper diam lobortis. Nunc at mauris volutpat, porta quam a, ultricies purus. Vivamus consectetur ligula sed neque fermentum, eu ultricies arcu convallis. Cras tincidunt magna id finibus cursus. Vestibulum at fringilla tellus, at facilisis dolor. Fusce mollis nisl non dui gravida, id congue est elementum. Nunc in metus varius, posuere felis et, hendrerit nisi.</p>
</main>
<footer>
<p>Copyright © 2022 My Website</p>
</footer>
</body>
</html>
```

PUTTING ALL OF THE SKILLS LEARNED IN THE COURSE INTO PRACTICE

Welcome to the final lesson of the "Learn HTML" course! Up to this point, you've learned the fundamentals of HTML and have gained the skills needed to create your own web pages and websites. In this lesson, we'll put all of these skills into practice by building a complete HTML website from scratch.

Before we begin, it's important to have a clear plan in place. This should include an outline of the content and structure of your website, as well as any design elements you want to include. It's also a good idea to sketch out a wireframe or create a mockup to visualize the layout of your website.

Example Project Outline

For this example project, we'll create a simple website for a fictional restaurant called "The Hungry Giraffe." The website will include information about the restaurant's menu, location, and hours, as well as a contact form for customers to make reservations.

First, we'll set up our development environment by installing a text editor and setting up a local server. Then, we'll create the basic HTML structure of the website, including the <html>, <head>, and <body> elements.

Next, we'll add content and structure to the website using HTML tags and attributes. This might include headings, paragraphs, lists, and images to provide information about the restaurant and its offerings.

We'll then use CSS to add style to the website, including colors, fonts, and layout elements to create a visually appealing and cohesive design.

Before publishing the website, we'll test and debug our code to ensure that everything is functioning properly and looks as intended on different browsers and devices.

Finally, we'll publish the website using a web hosting service or cloud platform like GitHub Pages.

HTML Code for the Project

Here is an example of the HTML code for the website:

```html
<!DOCTYPE html>
<html>
<head>
        <title>The Hungry Giraffe</title>
        <link rel="stylesheet" type="text/css" href="style.css">
</head>
<body>
        <header>
                <h1>The Hungry Giraffe</h1>
        </header>
        <nav>
                <ul>
                        <li><a href="#menu">Menu</a></li>
                        <li><a href="#location">Location</a></li>
                        <li><a href="#hours">Hours</a></li>
                        <li><a href="#contact">Contact</a></li>
                </ul>
        </nav>
        <main>
                <section id="menu">
                        <h2>Menu</h2>
                        <p>We offer a wide variety of delicious dishes, including sandwiches, salads, and entrees. Check out our full menu below:</p>
                        <ul>
                                <li>Grilled Cheese Sandwich</li>
                                <li>BLT Sandwich</li>
                                <li>Grilled Chicken Salad</li>
                                <li>Spaghetti Bolognese</li>
                        </ul>
                </section>
                <section id="location">
                        <h2>Location</h2>
                        <p>The Hungry Giraffe is located at 123 Main Street in Anytown, USA. We are open 7 days a week for lunch and dinner.</p>
                        <img src="map.jpg" alt="Map of The Hungry Giraffe's location">
                </section>
```

```html
<section id="hours">
    <h2>Hours</h2>
    <table>
        <tr>
            <th>Day</th>
            <th>Hours</th>
        </tr>
        <tr>
            <td>Monday</td>
            <td>11:00am - 9:00pm</
<section id="contact">
    <h2>Contact</h2>
    <p>Need to make a reservation or have a question about our menu? Contact us using the form below:</p>
    <form>
        <label for="name">Name:</label><br>
        <input type="text" id="name" name="name"><br>
        <label for="email">Email:</label><br>
        <input type="text" id="email" name="email"><br>
        <label for="message">Message:</label><br>
        <textarea id="message" name="message"></textarea><br>
        <input type="submit" value="Submit">
    </form>
</section>
</main>
<footer>
    <p>Copyright 2021 The Hungry Giraffe</p>
</footer>
</body>
</html>
```

This is just a basic example of the structure and content that could be included in a complete HTML website for a restaurant. With the skills learned in this course, you can use your creativity and knowledge of HTML to build more complex and customized websites for any purpose.

CSS Code for the Project

To add style to the website using CSS, we can create a separate stylesheet file called "style.css" and link to it in the <head> of our HTML file using the <link> element.

Here is an example of how we could use CSS to style the elements of our website:

```css
body {
    font-family: Arial, sans-serif;
    background-color: #f5f5f5;
    color: #333;
    margin: 0;
    padding: 0;
}
header {
    background-color: #fcba03;
    padding: 20px;
    text-align: center;
}
h1 {
    color: white;
    font-size: 2em;
    margin: 0;
}
nav {
    background-color: #333;
    color: white;
    display: flex;
    justify-content: space-between;
    padding: 20px;
}
nav ul {
    display: flex;
    list-style: none;
    margin: 0;
    padding: 0;
}
nav li {
    margin: 0 10px;
}
a {
    color: white;
```

```css
        text-decoration: none;
}
a:hover {
        color: #fcba03;
}
main {
        margin: 0 auto;
        max-width: 960px;
        padding: 20px;
}
section {
        margin-bottom: 20px;
}
h2 {
        color: #fcba03;
        font-size: 1.5em;
        margin-bottom: 10px;
}
img {
        max-width: 100%;
        height: auto;
}
table {
        border-collapse: collapse;
        width: 100%;
}
th, td {
        border: 1px solid #ccc;
        padding: 8px;
        text-align: left;
}
tr:nth-child(even) {
        background-color: #f2f2f2;
}
form {
        margin-bottom: 20px;
```

```css
}
label {
        display: block;
        font-size: 1.1em;
        margin-bottom: 5px;
}
input[type="text"], textarea {
        border: 1px solid #ccc;
        font-size: 1em;
        padding: 8px;
        width: 100%;
}
input[type="submit"] {
        background-color: #fcba03;
        border: none;
        color: white;
        cursor: pointer;
        font-size: 1em;
        padding: 10px;
        width: 100%;
}
input[type="submit"]:hover {
        background-color: #e3a800;
}
footer {
        background-color: #333;
        color: white;
        padding: 20px;
        text-align: center;
}
```

With these styles in place, our website should have a cohesive and visually appealing design.

Wrapping It Up

Before publishing the website, we'll want to test and debug our code to ensure that everything is functioning properly and looks as intended on different browsers and devices. This can be done by using a variety of tools such as browser developer consoles, online testing platforms, and responsive design testing tools.

We can also use a version control system like Git to track changes to our code and easily roll back any issues that may arise during the testing and debugging process.

Once we are confident that our website is ready to go live, we can publish it using a web hosting service or cloud platform like GitHub Pages. This will make our website accessible to the public via a unique URL.

Before publishing, it's also a good idea to optimize our website for search engines by including relevant keywords in the content and tags, and by making sure all of our links are working properly.

With these steps complete, our HTML website is ready for the world to see!

THANK YOU

Thank you again for choosing "Learn HTML". I hope it helps you in your journey to learn HTML and achieve your goals. Please take a small portion of your time and share this with your friends and family and write a review for this book. I hope your programming journey does not end here. If you are interested, check out other books that I have or find more coding challenges at: https://codeofcode.org